the Bowler's Meatball Cookbook

Jez Felwick is
The Bowler, delivering gourmet
meatballs, fish balls and veg balls from The Lawn
Ranger, his grass-fed van, that can be found in various
locations around the UK. All balled by hand, his Great Balls
of Fire have garnered fans (or ballers) from food critics to
fashionistas. Jez learnt to cook at the organic farm and cookery
school Ballymaloe near Cork before discovering the 'food truck'
scene on a trip to the US which inspired the launch of The Bowler.

Currently a regular on the London street food scene,
The Bowler also makes appearances at farmers' markets,
music events and summer festivals throughout the UK.
Find him on Twitter @TheBowlerUK, or online at
thebowleruk.tumblr.com.

the Bowler's
Meatball
Cookbook

Jez Felwick

Mitchell Beazley

For Mum and Dad,
with much love.

First published in Great Britain in 2013
by Mitchell Beazley,
an imprint of Octopus Publishing Group Ltd,
Endeavour House, 189 Shaftesbury Avenue,
London WC2H 8JY
www.octopusbooks.co.uk

An Hachette UK Company
www.hachette.co.uk

British Library Cataloguing-in-Publication Data.
A catalogue record for this book is available from the
British Library.

Publisher Alison Starling
Senior editor Sybella Stephens
Art direction and design Juliette Norsworthy
Illustrator Abigail Read
Photography Cristian Barnett
Home economist Annie Rigg
Recipe tester Catherine Phipps
Prop stylist Liz Belton
Production Lucy Carter

ISBN: 978 1 84533 749 0
Printed and bound in China

All recipes have been tested in metric.
Medium eggs and whole milk should be used,
unless otherwise stated.

Contents

Let's get the ball rolling ...

I feel privileged to have been given the opportunity to write this book at such an exciting time for food on the streets of the UK. It's been a year since I launched The Bowler. A year-long white-knuckle ride of big-dipping decisions, drops into the unknown and feeling the rush of serving people food I've created. Not to mention getting to grips with a whole host of regulations, legalities, financial fun times and new media. The side orders have involved dealing with the nerves, the stress, juggling my personal life, together with the sweat, tiredness and backache that come with the territory.

I was lucky to grow up surrounded and exposed to all sorts of food by a family who loved to cook, eat and entertain. Grandmothers from Devon and the East End of London who produced the best pasties and roasts, a mum with understated skills in the kitchen who can turn her hand to anything, as long as her trusty kitchen timers are to hand. Dad left the air force and worked his way up the food chain, becoming a very successful grocer. I used to eat everything, until my little brother Matt came along, I'm told, but after a few years on attention-seeking hunger strikes, I got back on the gravy train and have been eating ever since.

The Bowler wasn't a totally planned initiative, nor was it totally random. Several years back, I decided to have a four-month sabbatical from work and used the inheritance money my GM (grandma) had left me to go to Ballymaloe, a cookery school set on an organic farm near Cork in Ireland. The three months I spent there changed everything. Cooking gave me time to relax and provided me with a quiet time to focus, away from other distractions. I returned to London and looked for a way I could get involved with the farmers' market scene, which had been brought to my attention in Ireland. I hooked up with a Hertfordshire-based organic chicken and egg farmer, as I wanted to get hold of lots of chicken carcasses in order to make fresh stock for organic soup. I started working for the farmer, dropping off produce to be sold at various locations in London and then running the market stall in Clapham. Not only did I get an insight into how the farm was run, but it was a quick way to sell pots of homemade soup at various markets. As a weekend job this gave me an outlet to practise some of the things I'd learnt in Ireland. I ran the stalls and sold soup for many months before the real job, and life, distracted me again.

Cooking and the food business kept niggling at me, though. Then the 'food truck' scene in the US caught my attention. Amazing trucks selling the most delicious and varied food. I read, researched and took to the kitchen. I thought this could be the way to get into the marketplace without thousands of pounds of investment. When I was first thinking about the food I wanted to sell, I knew I wanted something that was easy to 'get'. Something that didn't need an explanation. Something that could have maximum flavour within it, but also within the sauce it came in. Then kapow! I was hit straight on. Not by a ball, but by a thought. Meatballs.

Everyone loves a meatball: the flavour combinations and possibilities are endless, they're fun, they're comforting, they conjure up all sorts of nostalgic childhood memories because people have grown up eating them, and almost every culture has its own variation – albóndigas, frikadelle, köttbullar, kofte, polpette, to name but a few. Meatballs and minced meat recipes are mentioned in the Roman cooking text *Apicius*, where it says that minced peacock is the best meat to use, followed by pheasant. My favourite peacock recipe will be in book two ...

The obsession began. I started grinding my own meat in search of the perfect ball, and entered London's emerging street food scene, as this was a reasonably affordable way to get to sell my food and get feedback. What started out by being a weekend passion-project-hobby-cum-trial really began to gain momentum. I was offered a spot to trade at a two-day music festival on Clapham Common. Page 1 of the catering handbook says: 'Don't trade at a 15,000-people-a-day festival for your first event.' However, Andy Ashton, the show's manager, was very persuasive: 'Look, it's a great opportunity to see what it's like trading at a festival with a really nice team of people, before you head out into the real world that's full of grouchy so and so's.' Fair point. I went looking for more 'No, don't be stupids' from Robin Bidgood of Smart Hospitality, a top London caterer. 'Sounds like a great idea, it would be a good test, we can help you I'm sure.' Not the answer I was looking for. Finally, as I tried to frame it as a risky and bad idea, Petra Barran of UK street food collective Eat.St merely said, 'Why wouldn't you do it?' I had effectively given myself an Apprentice-sized challenge to undertake single-handed ... with a little help from my friends. Four days of little or no sleep ensued. It was exhilarating.

I was chomping at the bit to get a van of some sort when the Lawn Ranger galloped straight on to eBay. Perfect. Well, sort of. Page 2 of the catering handbook says, 'Get a vehicle that is suited to your operation.' Not quite the case with the Lawn Ranger, but he's definitely a head-turner, and before long I was invited to be part of the massive Friday night street market The Long Table in Dalston, where 2,000 people turned up at a 500-capacity car park filled with a few food traders and a bar.

Food fanatic Twitter lovers started congregating @tweat_up's, and before long I was invited to feed the already full at the UK Chilli Stand Off, followed by a regular spot at the inaugural Brockley Market in south-east London. On each occasion I was honoured to attend, felt proud to be there and would always meet such great and positive people. The food streets aren't lined with gold, but the people you meet and the experiences are, which is why it is such a great thing to be involved with. I have met some amazing new people, all committed to the same cause and driven by similar passions. We've laughed along the way and been fed, well fed, on all levels.

It's taken me a while to get here, but there's nothing wrong with that. Sometimes things niggle away at us. It's hard to take that first step, to break the routine, to throw yourself into something new. Food had been that niggle. In fact, nibble might be more appropriate. Nibbling away, but being fed by the fear that doing something totally different would be foolish.

This book contains some of my favourite ball recipes to date. Balls that I have taken on the road, sold at the markets, as well as cooked at home. It provides you with ball skills for you to be able to adapt and create your own succulent spheres. But merely the fact that I have had the opportunity to write this shows anyone who is teetering on the brink of making a decision to jump into something new that it can only be a good thing. You may not make a mint in whatever you choose to do, but the experience you will have and people you meet will be priceless.

Life's about putting your balls on the line once in a while, but in the meantime read, roll, sauce, side, salad and support your local traders.

It's all about the meat

The problem with many ready-made meatballs is that they simply don't tell you exactly what cuts of meat they are made from. I also have a slight trust issue generally when it comes to minced meat. I've found that buying cheaper cuts of meat and mince from supermarkets yields different results. Ready-made mince will result in a tasty meatball, but you may notice that a lot of liquid and fat leaks out of the balls, and that they shrink. This could be down to a number of factors, but I have found that it doesn't happen with whole cuts of meat I have minced myself or bought from my butcher.

It was important for me to buy a variety of cuts of meat and actually mince them myself, but living in a one-bed flat in London didn't lend itself to storing vast amounts of kitchen equipment. Luckily my mum, Lynne, is a hoarder par excellence. A quick call to her and off I went to pick up her meat grinder. It turned out to be something she'd bought at a car boot sale decades ago – £3.18 according to the label. It was better looking, in a retro way, than it was practical, but it chewed its way though the first few pork shoulders and pieces of beef chuck I threw at it. Then I discovered a handy meat-grinding attachment for my KitchenAid and I was away.

I know that it may not be practical to mince your own meat, so I would urge you to get to know a butcher who will do it for you. Of course, every cookbook you read tells you to do this, but that's because it really is the best thing to do. Tell him you want to make the best meatballs in the world – that will trigger a conversation where he gives you his opinion, and you're off.

You have the beginnings of a relationship where you can bond over meat. I ask for my mince to be put through the machine twice to distribute the fat more evenly.

Provenance is key. Free-range and organic butchers should be able to trace each beast back to the field. Your butcher should know most about the quality, welfare and condition of the meat he gets, and where it's from. I was at my butcher's recently when I overheard him ending a relationship with a quality pork farmer because he had spotted that the fat content of the animals had been diminishing, signs that there could have been changes in their diet, age and welfare. It was a shame, as the supplier was down the road, but quality is quality. It was reassuring to witness this. All good butchers will have this level of commitment to the produce they buy and sell. I believe it is better to pay a little more in order to make sure that farmers are able to produce the best meat, in the best conditions, at a fair price for them, rather than being squeezed by the demands of having to produce a vast quantity at the lowest price.

Good meat shouldn't smell and it certainly shouldn't be discoloured or slimy. The best meats for meatballs are often not the most expensive cuts either. All the more reason that the meat in them should be the best it can be. Meatballs do, by their nature, lend themselves to making a smaller amount of meat go a long way. I've found the best cuts for making meatballs include pork and lamb shoulder as well as beef chuck steak, which is often labelled braising steak. These cuts are full of flavour and have a good level of both meat and fat.

Meatball basics

Meatballs are almost impossible to mess up. If you are using great ingredients to start with, at worst you will end up with a super-tasty meat sauce in the unlikely event that your balls disintegrate. After much research and experimentation into the elements that make up a great ball, I have identified some basic balling techniques that can be applied (although there is by no means a right or wrong here, so do experiment'):

I use breadcrumbs in most of my recipes. Japanese panko breadcrumbs, in particular, are dry, so they absorb the moisture and fat in meatballs, helping to stop the balls drying out, but they are also fairly rough, which gives the balls a rustic texture. I like this – I'm not a fan of balls that seem over-processed and smooth. For smaller numbers at home I will cut the crusts off some 1–2-day-old bread and blitz it in a food processor to get a fine crumb. The crumbs can be stored in an airtight container for up to a month.

Tearing bread and soaking it is a method championed by many and is a good idea if you think your ingredients could benefit from added moisture, and this method helps to add a certain lightness.

Shop-bought natural crumb is another alternative. Heading into the more left field carbohydrates, crushed crackers, oats and rice will all help to absorb moisture, retaining the flavour in the ball, as well as adding texture. I would stay away from anything that already has seasoning in it, as you want to be able to control that yourself.

Combinations of meat can be great to experiment with. Mixing pork with beef, with veal, with chicken and with prawns can be interesting. Throwing cured meats such as Serrano ham, bacon, chorizo into the mix leads to great results, and if you want to use a lean meat like venison, try adding a little straight pork fat or pork belly to aid flavour and moisture.

There are plenty of options for adding even more flavour to the meatballs. **Fresh and dried herbs give flavour and colour, as do chillies, spices, mustards and mayos.**

I always use eggs in the mix. I find they not only help to bind the ingredients together, but also add a level of fat and richness, giving a velvety texture.

The size of the meatballs is the next thing to think about. I mainly work to a 5cm diameter ball, which is about the size of a golfball and is the size I serve. I find packing a Disher ice cream scoop (number 20) with meat mix is enough for a 5cm ball each time, which can help speed up your balling considerably. In my recipes I give the cooking times for that size unless otherwise stated, but feel free to pick whatever size you want. The smaller the balls, the less time they need, so adjust the timings accordingly if you are making canapé-sized snacks.

When it comes to rolling, wet your hands to stop the mix sticking to them, and be sure to pack each ball firmly before rolling it between your palms.

Finally, the cooking method debate. Frying, braising, baking – each method has its merits. For the most part I bake my balls and will challenge any diehard 'pan-fry only' campaigners to come down and pan-fry a batch of 2,000 balls. Baking provides a controlled way of cooking the balls through evenly (if your oven is any good), after which you can add them to a sauce. Pan-frying in small batches does give the balls a delicious, caramelized outside, and deep-frying the balls in panko crumbs gives them a golden crunch. I have in most cases given instructions for baking the balls, but, again, feel free to change and experiment.

Resting the mixture for 30 minutes before cooking helps the ingredients and flavours mingle. Once a mixture is made it is fine to keep it in the fridge for 24 hours before cooking.

Once cooked, the balls can be refrigerated for up to 3 days and eaten cold or reheated either in a sauce, gently simmering for 15 minutes, or in a pan with 4 tablespoons of light stock. Alternatively you can reheat them for 20 minutes in the oven at 180°C (350°F), Gas Mark 4, or in a microwave (following user instructions). Balls can also be frozen for up to 2 months, but make sure you defrost them fully before reheating, taking extra care with poultry.

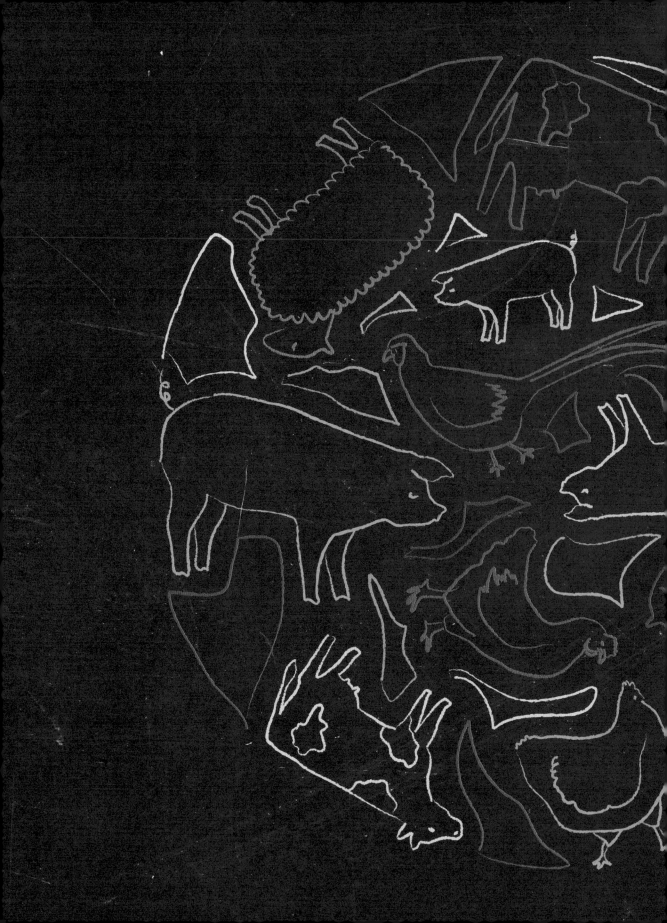

1. Meatballs

Serves
4–6

Pork & Fennel Meatballs

Pork and fennel is a classic Italian combination, and in meatballing circles they're in regular
contact. This is a recipe where I've decided to soak bread in milk, instead of using a dry crumb.
It helps give lightness to quite a dense mix.

**2 slices (about 100g) stale white
bread, crusts removed**

100ml milk

3 teaspoons fennel seeds

1 free-range egg

100g pancetta, finely chopped

500 pork shoulder, minced

1 onion, finely diced

**2 tablespoons chopped
flat-leaf parsley**

1 teaspoon salt

Preheat the oven to 220°C (425°F), Gas Mark 7 and line a large baking
tray with non-stick baking parchment.

Roughly tear up the bread and place it in a bowl. Pour over the milk
and set aside for 10–15 minutes.

Heat a heavy-based non-stick frying pan over a medium heat until it
begins to smoke, then add the fennel seeds. Toast them for around
30 seconds, or until they begin to brown and start to give off a fragrant
aroma. Grind them finely in a pestle and mortar.

Beat the egg in a large mixing bowl. Mash the bread and milk mixture
to a paste with a fork, then combine with the egg. Add all the other
ingredients and mix with your hands until well combined. This is a
pretty dense mix, so give it a good squeeze through your fingers to
make sure everything gets distributed evenly.

Heat a small frying pan over a high heat. Break off a small amount of
the mixture, flatten between your fingers and fry until cooked. Taste to
check the seasoning and add more salt if necessary. Form the mixture
into 16–18 balls each 5cm in diameter, packing each one firmly, and
place them on the prepared baking tray.

Bake for 15–18 minutes, turning the tray halfway through – the balls
should begin to brown on the top. Keep an eye on them to make sure
that they don't get burnt underneath.

Great served in a small crusty baguette, with Simple Tomato Sauce
(see page 99) and some mozzarella cheese melted on top.

A variation on this recipe is to go 'Pork 'n' Puy' – brown the balls in a pan,
rather than in the oven, then drop them into Puy lentils for 10 minutes
to finish cooking (see steps 1–2 on page 135 for how to cook lentils).
You may need to add a little more vegetable or chicken stock or water.
Garnish with shavings of Parmesan instead of mozzarella, and serve with
a side of crusty bread and butter.

Vietnamese Noodle Soup with Pork Balls

THE BALLS

1 large free-range egg

2 tablespoons plain flour

500g pork shoulder, minced

2 spring onions, finely sliced

1 tablespoon chopped coriander

2 tablespoons grated fresh ginger

3 tablespoons Nuoc Cham
(see page 119)

2 tablespoons olive oil

2.5 litres Chicken Stock (see page 90)

1 stick of cinnamon

4 spring onions, sliced lengthways

1 x 5cm piece of fresh ginger, peeled
and thinly sliced

2 teaspoons sugar

1 teaspoon salt

2 tablespoons fish sauce

1 star anise

200–300g rice vermicelli noodles
(allow 50g dried weight per person)

1 red Thai chilli, seeds removed
and sliced

2 tablespoons soy sauce

3 shallots, thinly sliced

150g beansprouts, blanched

Whenever I travel abroad now, I always try to factor in a visit to a local cooking class. It's a great way to get an insight into the food culture of a country, find out about new ingredients and come away with a few handy tips. I went to Vietnam on my honeymoon and couldn't move for pork balls, especially in soups, skewers and grilled. Here I have dropped some into a fairly traditional Vietnamese noodle soup that would be eaten day, night and even for breakfast.

Beat the egg with the plain flour in a large mixing bowl. Add the minced pork, spring onions, coriander, ginger and Nuoc Cham and mix with your hands until well combined.

Heat a small frying pan over a high heat. Break off a small amount of the mixture, flatten between your fingers and fry until cooked. Taste to check the seasoning and add more if necessary. Form the mixture into 16–18 balls each 4cm in diameter, packing each one firmly.

Heat the oil in a heavy-based frying pan and add the balls in batches so as not to overcrowd the pan. Brown the balls for 3 minutes on each side, then remove them from the pan and set aside.

In a large pan, add the Chicken Stock, cinnamon, spring onions, fresh ginger, sugar, salt, fish sauce and star anise, then bring to the boil. Reduce the heat and simmer for 40 minutes to let the flavours infuse. Strain the broth into another pan and taste for flavour – you can add a little Nuoc Cham if it needs a boost. Turn the heat back on, drop in the pork balls and simmer for 15 minutes, or until the balls are cooked through.

Meanwhile, drop the noodles into a pan of boiling water and cook for 2 minutes, then drain, refresh under cold water and drain again. Pour the soy sauce into a little dish and add the sliced chilli.

Drop the beansprouts into a saucepan of boiling water. Return to the boil and cook for 1 minute, then drain. Refresh in ice cold water and drain again.

Divide the noodles, shallots and beansprouts between your serving bowls, then pour over the broth and balls and garnish with coriander, basil and a wedge of lime. Serve the chilli soy sauce on the side to mix in if you require an extra flavour kick.

Serves
4–6

Mexballs

The slow-cooked Mexican dish pork carnitas is my favourite taco filling. Here I have taken a few of their ingredients and flavours and put them in the round. These Mexballs are great in a meatball burrito.

3 tablespoons olive oil

½ a small onion, very finely chopped

1 fennel bulb, finely diced

1 garlic clove, crushed

1 teaspoon ground cumin

1 teaspoon smoked paprika

½ teaspoon ground cinnamon

1 free-range egg

3 tablespoons double cream

500g pork shoulder, minced

2 tablespoons fresh lime juice

1 teaspoon dried chilli flakes

½ teaspoon chipotle paste

½ teaspoon dried oregano

3 tablespoons finely chopped coriander, including stalks

1 teaspoon salt

150g breadcrumbs

Preheat the oven to 220°C (425°F), Gas Mark 7 and line a large baking tray with non-stick baking parchment.

Heat the oil in a large heavy-based pan. Add the onion and fennel and cook over a low heat for 5 minutes. Add the garlic, cumin, smoked paprika and cinnamon and cook for a further 2 minutes, or until the onion is soft and translucent.

Break the egg into a large bowl, add the cream and whisk lightly with a fork. Add the minced pork, lime juice, chilli flakes, chipotle paste, oregano, coriander, salt and breadcrumbs, then add the onion and fennel mixture and mix with your hands until well combined.

Heat a small frying pan over a high heat. Break off a small amount of the mixture, flatten between your fingers and fry until cooked. Taste to check the seasoning and spice levels and add more if necessary. Form the mixture into about 18 meatballs each 5cm in diameter, packing each one firmly, and place them on the prepared baking tray.

Bake for 18–20 minutes, turning the tray halfway through – the balls should begin to brown on the top. Keep an eye on them to make sure that they don't get burnt underneath.

Serve in the Luardos Meatball Burrito (see page 22), or just on their own with Tomato Salsa and Cumin Soured Cream to dip (see pages 107 and 111), and tortilla chips to crunch on.

Serves
6

Luardos Meatball Burrito

I first met Simon Luard of Luardos at a pop-up chilli cooking competition hosted by @tweat_up. It was in the Tramshed in Shoreditch, where Mark Hix now has his restaurant. We were both parked indoors; The Lawn Ranger was opposite Simon's pink, graffiti-covered van Mary, which was luring the overfed to try a fish taco. Luardos also serve Mexican burritos out of Mary, as well as from Jesus which is parked at Whitecross Street Market (Whitecross Street has a great selection of top food traders, if you have a spare lunchtime in London and want to treat your tastebuds.) It wasn't long before we started experimenting with a few meatball burrito combos, and Simon has let me in on all the elements that make up the perfect burrito. Enjoy. A warning: start your beans the day before.

250g black turtle beans, soaked overnight

500g long-grain rice

10 tablespoons Monterey Jack cheese or medium Cheddar, grated

12 Mexballs (see page 21), cooked and warmed through

6 tablespoons chopped coriander

400ml Chipotle Tomato Sauce (see page 98)

6 tablespoons Tomato Salsa (see page 107)

12 tablespoons Guacamole (see page 104)

½ a white cabbage, finely shredded

6 tablespoons soured cream

6 large flour tortillas

sea salt

Drain the soaked beans, then cook them in fresh water until they are soft, about an hour once the water is boiling. Season with sea salt after they are cooked, not before or during, otherwise the beans won't soften.

Meanwhile, cook the rice according to the packet instructions.

Now get all the ingredients in a line so that they are easy to add to the tortillas in the right order. For us it goes: cheese, rice, black beans, meatballs, chopped coriander, chipotle tomato sauce, tomato salsa, guacamole, cabbage and soured cream.

Toast a tortilla in a large dry frying pan until slightly brown but not crispy (it still needs to be pliable for wrapping). Add the grated cheese while it's toasting, to start it melting.

One by one, add the burrito ingredients – we've suggested some amounts, but really, just add as much or as little as you prefer. Once it's all done, either wrap it up in foil or put it as it is on a plate and eat it before it all falls apart – it's probably going to get messy. Make the rest of the burritos the same way.

Best served with a cold beer and a roll of kitchen towel.

Serves
6

Balls on the Line

This is the best way to prepare meatballs for the barbecue, and can be used for all the different types. Make sure you soak the wooden skewers in water before you use them, otherwise they will catch fire …

2 tablespoons olive oil

3 shallots, finely diced

2 garlic cloves, crushed

100g ricotta cheese

1 large free-range egg

2 tablespoons double cream

500g beef chuck steak, minced

100g breadcrumbs

2 tablespoons wholegrain mustard

2 teaspoons chopped thyme

¼ teaspoon dried chilli flakes

salt and freshly ground black pepper

Fire up the barbecue and place 6 wooden skewers in water to soak. Alternatively, after making the balls, turn the grill on, or preheat the oven to 220°C (425°F), Gas Mark 7, and line a baking tray with non-stick baking parchment.

Heat the oil in a heavy-based pan and add the shallots and a good pinch of salt and pepper. Cook over a low heat for 3 minutes, then add the garlic and cook for another 3 minutes, or until the shallots are soft and translucent.

Put the ricotta, egg and cream into a large bowl and mix together, breaking up the lumps of ricotta.

Add the shallots and garlic to the ricotta mix along with the minced beef, breadcrumbs, mustard, thyme, dried chilli flakes and 1 teaspoon of salt, and mix with your hands until well combined.

Heat a small frying pan over a high heat. Break off a small amount of the mixture, flatten between your fingers and fry until cooked. Taste to check the seasoning and add more salt and chilli if necessary. Form the mixture into 18 meatballs each about 5cm in diameter, packing each one firmly, then thread 3 on to each skewer.

Leave to chill and firm up in the fridge for 30 minutes, then brush with a little olive oil and grill on the barbecue, turning the skewers as you go so that the balls cook through evenly and brown up on the outside. Alternatively, you can cook them under the grill, or put them on the prepared baking tray and bake in the oven for 15–20 minutes, turning the tray halfway through and keeping an eye on them to make sure that they don't get burnt underneath.

Delicious with mustard or horseradish mayonnaise and a crunchy salad.

Serves
6

Ball Shiitake

Beef and mushrooms is a classic combination, and the meatiness of shiitake mushrooms works really well in a meatball. Make sure you cook the mushrooms well and good to extract their high water content. When you have a lot of mushrooms it's best to cook them in batches – if you overcrowd the pan they can become waterlogged.

15g butter

1 large onion, finely chopped

1 tablespoon runny honey

1 teaspoon cider vinegar

300g shiitake mushrooms, finely chopped

1 garlic clove, crushed

2 large free-range eggs

1kg beef chuck steak, finely minced

150g ricotta cheese

1 tablespoon finely chopped thyme

1 tablespoon finely chopped flat-leaf parsley

125g breadcrumbs

4 tablespoons milk

sea salt and freshly ground black pepper

Preheat the oven to 220ºC (425ºF), Gas Mark 7 and line 2 large baking trays with non-stick baking parchment.

Put a heavy-based frying pan over a medium heat and add the butter. Heat until it starts to foam, then add the onions and a good pinch of salt and pepper. Cook over a low heat for 5 minutes, then add the honey and vinegar and cook slowly for a further 10 minutes, or until the onion is soft, sticky and translucent.

Add the mushrooms and garlic to the pan, stir and cook for 7–10 minutes, or until the mushrooms begin to brown and any liquid has evaporated. Remove the pan from the heat and set aside to cool.

Beat the eggs in a large mixing bowl, then mix in the minced beef, the cooled mushroom and onion mix, the ricotta, thyme, parsley, breadcrumbs, milk and 2 teaspoons of salt.

Heat a small frying pan over a high heat. Break off a small amount of the mixture, flatten between your fingers and fry until cooked. Taste to check the seasoning and add more salt if necessary. Form the mixture into 18 balls each about 4–5cm in diameter, packing each one firmly, and place them on the prepared baking trays.

Bake in the oven for 15–20 minutes, turning the tray round halfway through – the balls should begin to brown on top. Keep an eye on them to make sure that they don't get burnt underneath.

Serve with Asian Greens (see page 152), and rice or noodles.

Serves
6–8

Beef & Chorizo Balls

Chorizo is one of my favourite ingredients. I love it. Sweet, spicy and smoky.
I will keep a cooking chorizo on hand to add to just about anything, in order to take it to the
next level. A starter for ten is to finely slice or dice it, fry it until crispy and use it like a
crouton on soups, salads and in sandwiches. It makes a great partner to beef, so it was thrown
into the mixer for this recipe early on.

2 tablespoons olive oil

2 shallots, finely chopped

1 garlic clove, crushed

1 large free-range egg

500g beef chuck steak, minced

**200g cooking chorizo, sweet or spicy,
finely diced**

**400g white rice, cooked weight
(100g uncooked)**

**200g Manchego cheese,
coarsely grated**

1 teaspoon smoked paprika

100g breadcrumbs

grated zest of 1 lemon

1 teaspoon salt

3 tablespoons chopped parsley

Preheat the oven to 220°C (425°F), Gas Mark 7 and line 2 baking trays with
non-stick baking parchment.

Heat the oil in a large heavy-based pan. Add the shallots and cook on a low
heat for 2 minutes. Add the garlic and cook for another 5 minutes, or until
the shallots are soft and translucent.

Beat the egg in a large bowl. Add the minced beef, shallots, garlic, chorizo,
rice, cheese, smoked paprika, breadcrumbs, lemon zest, salt and parsley
and mix with your hands until well combined.

Heat a small frying pan over a high heat. Break off a small amount of the
mixture, flatten between your fingers and fry until cooked. Taste to check
the seasoning and add more if necessary. Form the mixture into 28–30 balls
each about 5cm in diameter, packing each one firmly, and place them on
the prepared baking trays.

Bake for 18–20 minutes, turning the trays halfway through – the balls
should begin to brown on the top. Keep an eye on them to make sure
that they don't get burnt underneath.

I often serve these Bap 'n' Ball style. Get a bread roll of your choosing
(I like a toasted ciabatta or brioche burger bun). Then spread on some
Confit Garlic Mayonnaise (see page 115), add some green leaves (rocket,
etc), sliced gherkins or Pickled Cucumber (see page 148), and some
cheese you can melt under a grill or grate on top. Devour, but be sure
to have some napkins to hand.

Serves
4–6

Sweaty Balls

Quite simply, these balls are going to make you sweat.
A stalwart of the London street food scene, 'The Rib Man', aka Mark Gevaux, has been selling
his barbecue baby back ribs on London's Brick Lane and round about with huge success.
I love his mind-blowing Holy Fuck Hot Sauce, which is made from a combination of Scotch
Bonnet and Naga Jolokia chilli peppers. Here it gives the balls a boom, with the Cheddar
flavour following once the heat subsides.

1–2 tablespoons olive oil

½ an onion, finely chopped

1 garlic clove, crushed

30g tomato purée

2 free-range eggs

120g Cheddar cheese,
coarsely grated

500g beef chuck steak, minced

100g breadcrumbs

1 teaspoon salt

3 tablespoons finely chopped
oregano

3 tablespoons finely chopped
flat-leaf parsley

3 tablespoons (or to taste)
of The Rib Man's Holy Fuck
Hot Sauce (available from
www.theribman.co.uk)

Preheat the oven to 220°C (425°F), Gas Mark 7 and line a large baking
tray with non-stick baking parchment.

Heat the oil in a large heavy-based pan. Add the onion and cook on a
low heat for 2 minutes. Add the garlic and cook on a low heat for 3 more
minutes, or until the onion is translucent, then add the tomato purée and
keep cooking and stirring for 2 minutes.

Remove from the heat and allow to cool a little. Beat the eggs in a large
mixing bowl and add all the rest of the ingredients. Mix with your hands
until well combined.

Heat a small frying pan over a high heat. Break off a small amount of the
mixture, flatten between your fingers and fry until cooked. Taste to check
the seasoning and spiciness and add more if necessary. Form the mixture
into about 18 meatballs each 5cm in diameter, packing each one firmly,
and place them on the prepared tray.

Bake for 15–18 minutes, turning the tray halfway through – the balls
should begin to brown on the top. Keep an eye on them to make sure that
they don't get burnt underneath.

I suggest having some Cumin Soured Cream (see page 111) or Greek
yoghurt on standby to put the flames out, and wearing a towelling headband
to catch that perspiration.

Serves
4–6

Sticky Balls

These balls are sticky because of the sweet honey and garlic sauce they are served with, which makes them perfect for little ballers. Try getting the kids to wrap these balls inside an Iceberg lettuce leaf, to get some fresh vegetable crunch down them.

3 tablespoons olive oil

1 onion, finely chopped

1 tablespoon tomato purée

2 free-range eggs

250g pork shoulder, minced

250g beef chuck steak, minced

4 garlic cloves, crushed

1 tablespoon Dijon mustard

1 tablespoon Worcestershire sauce

150g breadcrumbs

2 teaspoons sea salt

1 x recipe Honey & Garlic Sticky
Ball Sauce (see page 96)

chopped chives, to garnish

Preheat the oven to 220°C (425°F), Gas Mark 7 and line a large baking tray with non-stick baking parchment.

To make the balls, heat the oil in a heavy-based pan over a medium heat. Add the onions, turn the heat to low and cook for 5 minutes until it turns translucent. Add the tomato purée and cook for a further 2 minutes. Set aside to cool.

Beat the eggs in a large bowl, then add the minced pork and beef, garlic, mustard, Worcestershire sauce, breadcrumbs and salt, and mix with your hands until well combined.

Heat a small frying pan over a high heat. Break off a small amount of the mixture, flatten between your fingers and fry until cooked. Taste to check the seasoning and add more if necessary. Form the mixture into about 20 balls each 5cm in diameter, packing each one firmly, and place them on the prepared baking tray.

Bake for 15–18 minutes, turning the tray halfway through – the balls should begin to brown on the top. Keep an eye on them to make sure that they don't get burnt underneath.

Heat the sauce through gently in a large saucepan. Add the balls and simmer for 2 minutes, then serve, topped with chives.

Some Pickled Carrot & Daikon (see page 148) is nice on the side, to cut through the sweetness.

Serves
4–6

Great Balls of Fire

This is the first ball I developed, and the first ball that I served to a member of the paying public. That was the moment when things really started to roll, with my cooking truly exposed and the adrenaline pumping. It felt good. This is a ball with plenty of flavour and texture, and I like to load up the chilli to increase the fire. The balls can take a good braise in any sauce, but I serve them in my spiced red onion and tomato version.

100g ricotta cheese

2 free-range eggs

400g pork shoulder, finely minced

200g beef chuck steak, finely minced

100g Japanese panko breadcrumbs or fresh breadcrumbs

2 garlic cloves, crushed

3 tablespoons finely chopped coriander stems, leaves reserved

2 teaspoons sea salt

½ teaspoon dried chilli flakes

1 x recipe Spiced Red Onion & Tomato Sauce (see page 100)

Preheat the oven to 220°C (425°F), Gas Mark 7 and line a large baking tray with non-stick baking parchment.

Put the ricotta into a large bowl and fork through to break it up. Add the eggs and whisk together. Add the minced pork and beef, panko crumbs (or breadcrumbs), garlic, coriander stems, salt and chilli flakes, and mix with your hands until well combined.

Heat a small frying pan over a high heat. Break off a small amount of the mixture, flatten between your fingers and fry until cooked. Taste to check the seasoning and spice levels and add more salt and chilli flakes if necessary. Form the mixture into about 18 balls each 4–5cm in diameter, packing each one firmly, and place them on the prepared baking tray.

Bake in the oven for 15–18 minutes, turning the tray round halfway through – the balls should begin to brown on the top. Keep an eye on them to make sure that they don't get burnt underneath.

Meanwhile, heat the sauce in a large pan over a medium heat. When the balls are cooked, add them to the sauce and simmer for 15 minutes.

Serve with soured cream on the side and a few leaves of coriander scattered on top, and a baby spinach and rocket salad.

Serves
4–6

The Popeye

Who likes spinach? Who's been brought up thinking it has superhuman properties?
Popeye had a lot to do with instilling that belief in me. In fact, my great-grandfather was a
sailor and had tattoos just like him. So this ball goes out to the spinach lovers. I use fresh
spinach here, rather than Popeye's tinned stuff. I also find it easier to eat with a fork rather
than sucking through a pipe … but each to their own.

400g fresh spinach leaves

2 tablespoons olive oil

1 large onion, finely chopped

2 garlic cloves, crushed

1 large free-range egg

2 tablespoons milk

65g fresh breadcrumbs

50g Parmesan cheese, finely grated

**2 tablespoons finely chopped
flat-leaf parsley**

**2 tablespoons finely chopped
fresh oregano, or 1 teaspoon
dried oregano**

300g pork shoulder, minced

300g beef chuck steak, minced

**sea salt and freshly ground
black pepper**

Preheat the oven to 220°C (425°F), Gas Mark 7 and line a large baking
tray with non-stick baking paper.

Wash the spinach, then place it in a large pan and add a splash of water.
Cook over a high heat, stirring, until the spinach has wilted and softened.
Squeeze it between two plates to get rid of any excess liquid, then chop
it finely.

Put the olive oil into a heavy-based frying pan over a medium heat. Add
the onion, garlic, black pepper and 2 teaspoons of salt. Stir over a low heat
for 6 minutes, or until the onion becomes translucent, taking care not to
burn the garlic (add a splash more oil if things look like they are sticking).
Add the spinach and cook, stirring, for a further 2 minutes. Then remove
from the heat and leave to cool to room temperature.

Beat together the egg and milk in a large mixing bowl, then add the
breadcrumbs, Parmesan, parsley, oregano and a pinch of salt and stir to
combine. Add the minced pork and beef and the onion mixture, then mix
with your hands until well combined.

Heat a small frying pan over a high heat. Break off a small amount of the
mixture, flatten between your fingers and fry until cooked. Taste to check
the seasoning and add more salt and pepper if necessary. Form the mixture
into about 20 meatballs each 5cm in diameter, packing each one firmly, and
place them on the prepared baking tray.

Bake for 15–20 minutes, turning the tray round halfway through – the balls
should begin to brown on the top. Keep an eye on them to make sure that
they don't get burnt underneath.

Serve the balls with Simple Tomato Sauce on the side for dipping
(see page 99), or with mustard mashed potato and a green salad.

Makes
6–7

Homeslice Meatball Calzone

In their own words, 'Homeslice is the love-child of three men with a passion for making and eating woodfired pizza.' I met this Kiwi threesome early on in Bowler life. Hugging their homemade wood-fired oven-cum-trailer is a great way to keep warm on a cold evening. Their pizzas are stunning – light with a crisp base – and I'm thrilled they've shared a little doughy delight here.

250ml warm water

20g soft brown sugar

7g dried yeast

600g bread flour

10g sea salt (Maldon recommended)

100g butter, melted

6–7 cooked Bowler meatballs and sauce of your choice

freshly grated mozzarella cheese

sliced spring onions

Put the water into a bowl and add the sugar. Stir until dissolved, then add the yeast and cover the bowl. Leave for 5 minutes, until the yeast is creamy.

Put the flour and salt into a mixing bowl and stir in the melted butter and the yeast mixture. Once the mixture becomes a dough ball, place it on a floured board. Knead well for 10–15 minutes (don't slack!), adding more flour as needed. The dough shouldn't stick to your hands but should cling to itself – the more you mix it the wetter it will feel. Once kneaded, place the dough back in the bowl and cover with a cloth. Let it sit in a warm place for 40 minutes or so, until it has almost doubled in size.

Divide the risen dough into 6 or 7 portions and roll each into a tight sphere. Place the balls on a tray, cover with clingfilm, and put the tray in a cool place for an hour. It will now be ready to roll out, but your window for use is getting small. If you are making your dough earlier in the day you can keep the balls in the fridge, but bring them out about 20–30 minutes before use.

Heat the oven to 220°C (425°F), Gas Mark 7. Flour your board and if you're a hands-on person you can stretch and roll the dough into a circle using your hands; however, using a rolling pin is a viable option. Roll the dough as thin as you can without splitting it, making circles 15–20cm across and 5mm deep.

Place a meatball on one half of your dough circle, adding the sauce of your choice. I recommend the Beef & Chorizo Ball (see page 28) with Chipotle Tomato Sauce (see page 98). Spinkle over some grated mozzarella and fresh spring onions. To seal the calzone, take a brush or your finger and spread sauce thinly around the edge of the dough circle. Fold the empty half of the circle over the filling, press together and pinch the edges – the better the seal here the more it will puff and look delicious.

Place the calzones on a baking tray. Bake for 5–10 minutes, or until starting to colour. Don't leave them too long or you'll end up with dry calzone. Serve straight from the oven. They're best served as a small starter. Enjoy.

Serves
5–6

Smokin' Bacon Balls

There were four hours to go before I was expected at a private party Richard Bacon was throwing
in his back garden, for which I'd been asked to do the food. Exciting stuff. I had some chuck steak
in the fridge along with some smoked lardons. 'Rude not to', I thought, turning the oven on.

1 tablespoon olive oil

200g oak-smoked bacon lardons

150g breadcrumbs

2 free-range eggs

100ml double cream

200g ricotta cheese

750g beef chuck steak, minced

**150g Applewood smoked Cheddar,
coarsely grated**

1 teaspoon smoked paprika

2 teaspoons salt

**2 tablespoons chopped
flat-leaf parsley**

Preheat the oven to 220°C (425°F), Gas Mark 7 and line 2 large baking trays
with non-stick baking parchment. If you don't have two trays, you will need
to cook the balls in batches.

Heat the oil in a large heavy-based pan. Add the bacon lardons and cook
on a medium heat for 5 minutes, or until they are crispy.

Put the breadcrumbs into a mixing bowl. Remove the lardons from the pan
to a board and pour the juices and oil from the pan into the breadcrumbs.
Chop the lardons finely, then add them to the crumb mix and allow to cool.

Beat the eggs and cream in a large mixing bowl, then add the ricotta,
mixing to break up any large lumps. Add the rest of the ingredients and
mix with your hands until well combined.

Heat a small frying pan over a high heat. Break off a small amount of the
mixture, flatten between your fingers and fry until cooked. Taste to check
the seasoning and the smokiness and add more salt, pepper and paprika
if necessary. Form the mixture into 30 balls each 5cm in diameter, packing
each one firmly, and place them on the prepared baking trays.

Bake for 15–18 minutes, turning the trays halfway through – the balls
should begin to brown on the top. Keep an eye on them to make sure that
they don't get burnt underneath.

A delicious way to gain weight, served with a Simple Tomato Sauce (see
page 99) and a slab of Potato Rösti (see page 131), or try them with a fried
egg and some Wild Mushroom Sauce (see page 92) or hollandaise.

Serves
5–6

Hawksmoor's Meatballs & Grits

Hawksmoor, in my opinion, is the best steak restaurant in London.
It's all about the meat, with complete commitment to finding the best British cuts
available. This is also at the heart of great meatballing. I've followed Hawksmoor
owners Huw and Will's rise to the top of the meaty food chain, I've listened to
their advice, as well as their sublime karaoke singing, and I'm thrilled that they
have let me have their own meatball recipe.
Grits are very similar to polenta, made from a coarse-ground corn. They were
originally associated with Native Americans and are often eaten in the US for
breakfast, much like porridge is in the UK.

1 large free-range egg, beaten

500g minced pork

500g minced beef

1 garlic clove, chopped

50ml white wine

50g Stilton cheese, grated

50g plain flour, for dusting

olive oil, for frying

sea salt and freshly ground
black pepper

TO GARNISH

10 sage leaves

a handful of large capers

Preheat the oven to 150°C (300°F), Gas Mark 2.

To make the meatballs, beat the egg in a large bowl. Mix in the minced
meat, garlic, egg, wine, Stilton, salt and pepper. Form the mixture into
25 balls each 5cm in diameter, and dust each one with a little flour.

Fry the balls in oil for about 15 minutes, or until golden – do this in
several batches – if you overcrowd the frying pan it will be hard to
get them to brown evenly, and they may break up when you are
turning them. Once cooked, place the balls in a deep casserole.

THE SAUCE

1 small onion, chopped

25g or 5 large, fat garlic cloves, crushed

½ a red chilli, roughly chopped

1 carrot, chopped

2 tablespoons olive oil

500ml chicken gravy (chicken stock reduced by half)

500ml beef gravy (beef stock reduced by half)

500g tinned chopped tomatoes

In the same pan, fry the onion, garlic, chilli and carrot in 2 tablespoons of olive oil and add them to the casserole with the meatballs. Pour over the chicken and beef gravies and the chopped tomatoes, then season to taste with salt and pepper. Place over a medium heat and bring to a simmer, then place in the oven for 1 hour. Taste and correct the seasoning if necessary.

Remove the meatballs from the casserole and keep warm. Pass the sauce through a chinoise or blend with an immersion blender, then combine the sauce and meatballs and set aside in a warm place until ready to serve.

Just before serving, fry the sage leaves and capers in a little olive oil over a high heat until crisp.

To serve, place a spoonful of cheese grits or polenta in the base of a bowl and top with the hot meatballs and a little sauce. Garnish with the fried sage leaves and capers (turn the page to see the finished result).

CHEESE GRITS

1.2 litres milk

250g white grits or white polenta

100g butter

100g Doddington cheese, grated

100g Ogleshield cheese, grated

To make the cheese grits, heat the milk to a simmer in a large pan. Pour the grits or polenta into the milk in a steady stream, whisking as you go. Reduce the heat and stir steadily for 20 minutes, then stir in the butter followed by the two cheeses. Keep stirring until smooth.

Set aside and keep warm until needed.

Serves
4–6

Björn Balls

My great friend Chris fell in love with a Swedish girl, Annika. The downsides were he moved to
Sweden, almost became teetotal because of the price of booze and can now speak about us
behind our backs in Swedish. The upsides are that I regularly go to one of the meatball capitals
of the world, get forced to drink tasty schnapps and have a free place to stay. There is a lot of
discussion about what makes a traditional Swedish 'köttbullar'. This recipe contains a mix
of some of my findings but I am not going to claim it's 100% traditional. It tastes great though.

2 tablespoons olive oil

1 small onion, finely diced

1 large free-range egg

300g minced beef

150g minced pork

150g minced veal

100g dried breadcrumbs

4 tablespoons milk

1 tablespoon juice from tinned
Abba anchovies (optional)

¼ teaspoon ground allspice

¼ teaspoon ground nutmeg

a pinch of ground ginger

½ teaspoon freshly ground
black pepper

1½ teaspoons salt

Preheat the oven to 220°C (425°F), Gas Mark 7 and line a large baking tray
with non-stick baking parchment.

Heat the oil in a large heavy-based pan. Add the onion and cook on a low heat
for 5 minutes, or until the onion is soft and translucent. At this stage, I would
always add a few pinches of salt and grinds of pepper so the onions are
seasoned from the start, meaning that you don't have to add so much later.

Beat the egg in a large bowl. Add the minced beef, pork and veal, the
breadcrumbs, milk, anchovy juice (if using), allspice, ground nutmeg,
ginger, pepper and salt and mix with your hands until well combined.

Heat a small frying pan over a high heat. Break off a small amount of the
mixture, flatten between your fingers and fry until cooked. Taste to check
the seasoning and add more if necessary. Form the mixture into about
18 balls each 5cm in diameter, packing each one firmly, and place them
on the prepared baking tray.

Bake for 18–20 minutes, turning the tray halfway through – the balls
should begin to brown on the top. Keep an eye on them to make sure that
they don't get burnt underneath. Let them rest for 2 minutes and they are
good to go. Alternatively, brown the balls in olive oil over a high heat for
8–10 minutes, then drop them into a pan of simmering Crispy Cream Sauce
(see page 102) to finish cooking.

Traditionally, Swedish meatballs are served with boiled or mashed potatoes,
lingonberry jam (if you can't get hold of lingonberry, use cranberry),
cream sauce, sliced pickled cucumber and fresh dill, but they taste great
with almost anything.

Serves
4–6

Côte de Veau Pojarski

Whilst researching different balling ideas, I came across a classic French dish called Côte de Veau Pojarski where the meat is removed from veal chops, minced, balled and reformed round the bone. Russian in its origin, the story goes that Pojarski, a 19th-century Russian inn keeper, made his name by making tasty beef meatballs loved by Tsar Nicholas. One day the Tsar dropped by but there was no beef, so the dish was improvised using veal, which the Tsar loved even more. Serve these for the Tsars in your life.

4–6 veal chop bones (depending on how many you are serving)

50g butter

3 banana shallots, finely diced

1 garlic clove, crushed

1 large free-range egg

150ml double cream

500g British rose veal, minced

100g breadcrumbs

3 tablespoons finely chopped chives

1 tablespoon chopped flat-leaf parsley

1 teaspoon chopped thyme

¼ teaspoon freshly grated nutmeg

1 teaspoon salt

¼ teaspoon black pepper

1 lemon, zest finely grated

Put the veal chop bones into a pan of boiling water for 10 minutes, then scrape everything off them so that they are clean and leave them to dry.

Preheat the oven to 220°C (425°F), Gas Mark 7.

Heat 20g of the butter in a large heavy-based pan. Add the shallots and cook on a low heat for 2 minutes. Add the garlic and cook for a further 5 minutes, or until the shallots are soft and translucent. Set aside to cool slightly.

Break the egg into a large bowl, add the cream and whisk lightly with a fork. Add the cooked shallots and garlic, minced veal, breadcrumbs, chives, parsley, thyme, nutmeg, lemon zest, salt and pepper and mix with your hands until well combined.

Heat a small frying pan over a high heat. Break off a small amount of the mixture, flatten between your fingers and fry until cooked. Taste to check the seasoning and add more if necessary. Form the mixture into 4–6 big balls, then make a hole in each with a knife and insert a veal bone, pushing and firming the mixture around the bone.

Melt the remaining butter and pour it into an ovenproof dish. Transfer the balls to the dish and bake for 30 minutes, basting with the butter and turning the dish halfway through – the balls should begin to brown on the top. Keep an eye on them to make sure that they don't get burnt underneath.

When the balls are cooked, take care transferring them from the dish to serving plates – support them underneath to make sure they don't split.

Mushrooms are a traditional accompaniment, so serve these balls with Wild Mushroom Sauce (see page 92), celeriac mash or some buttered pasta, and lemon wedges on the side.

Serves
4–6

The Rose Bowl

The consumption of veal has long been on the animal welfare agenda. However, I feel strongly that we should eat British rose veal, otherwise male calves are being killed and destroyed for no reason, the by-product of the milk industry, unable to give milk and not from herds bred for meat. They are reared in high welfare conditions approved by the RSPCA, so it seems an injustice not to put the meat to good use.

50g butter

3 banana shallots, finely diced

1 garlic clove, crushed

2 free-range eggs

400g British rose veal, minced

100g pork shoulder, minced

50g Parmesan cheese, grated

1 tablespoon chopped
flat-leaf parsley

1 tablespoons finely chopped
oregano

1 teaspoon salt

¼ teaspoon black pepper

finely grated zest of 1 lime

150g breadcrumbs

100ml milk

Preheat the oven to 220°C (425°F), Gas Mark 7 and line a large baking tray with non-stick baking parchment.

Heat 25g of the butter in a large heavy-based pan. Add the shallots and cook on a low heat for 2 minutes. Add the garlic and cook for a further 5 minutes, or until the shallots are soft and translucent. Towards the end of the cooking time add the remaining 25g of butter and let it melt, then set aside to cool slightly.

Beat the eggs in a large bowl. Add the minced veal and pork, Parmesan, parsley, oregano, salt, pepper and lime zest. Stir the breadcrumbs and milk into the onions and butter, then add to the meat mixture and mix with your hands until well combined.

Heat a small frying pan over a high heat. Break off a small amount of the mixture, flatten between your fingers and fry until cooked. Taste to check the seasoning and add more if necessary. Form the mixture into 18–20 balls each 5cm in diameter, packing each one firmly, and place them on the prepared baking tray.

Bake for 18–20 minutes, turning the tray halfway through – the balls should begin to brown on the top. Keep an eye on them to make sure that they don't get burnt underneath.

If you need comforting, serve the balls with Wild Mushroom Sauce (see page 92), Polenta (see page 126) and green beans, or lighten them up for summer with a courgette and pine nut salad.

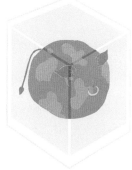

Serves
4–6

Green Chilli Chicken Balls

I love these balls because you can really taste the green chilli in them – it adds a great freshness. I use chicken thighs here because they have much more flavour and the result is a lot more moist compared to using breast meat, which can sometimes dry out too quickly.

2 tablespoons olive oil

1 onion, finely chopped

2 garlic cloves, crushed

8 fresh green chillies, seeds removed, finely chopped

1 x 4cm piece of fresh ginger, peeled and chopped

20 cashew nuts

3 tablespoons finely chopped coriander, plus extra leaves to garnish

2 free-range eggs

2 tablespoons milk

750g boneless chicken thighs, minced

2 teaspoons Garam Masala (see page 111)

150g breadcrumbs

2 teaspoons salt

freshly ground black pepper

lime wedges, to serve

Preheat the oven to 220°C (425°F), Gas Mark 7 and line a large baking tray with non-stick baking parchment.

Heat the oil in a large heavy-based pan. Add the onion and cook on a low heat for 2 minutes. Add the garlic, chillies, ginger and cashew nuts and cook on a low heat for 3 more minutes, or until the onion is translucent.

Remove from the heat, allow to cool a little, then put into a food processor with the coriander and blitz to a rough paste. You might have to add a splash of olive oil or water to help it blend properly. Beat the eggs with the milk in a large bowl, then add the paste, minced chicken, garam masala, breadcrumbs, salt and pepper, and mix well.

Heat a small frying pan over a high heat. Break off a small amount of the mixture, flatten between your fingers and fry until cooked. Taste to check the seasoning and add more salt and spices if necessary. Form the mixture into 20–22 meatballs about 5cm in diameter, packing each one firmly, and place them on the prepared baking tray.

Bake for 15–18 minutes, turning the tray halfway through – the balls should begin to brown on the top. Keep an eye on them to make sure that they don't get burnt underneath.

Serve with Coconut Curry Sauce (see page 117) and steamed jasmine rice with lime wedges on the side. Garnish with Crispy Fried Shallots (see page 154) and coriander leaves.

Serves
4–6

Steamy Chicken Balls

It's time to dust off your bamboo steamer – you know it's on the top shelf somewhere.
This is my ball food answer to Chinese dumplings. Am convinced they're very good for you.
Anything steamed is, right?

1 large free-range egg

3 spring onions, finely sliced

2 garlic cloves, crushed

200g skinless, boneless chicken breasts, minced

300g skinless, boneless chicken thighs, minced

1 x 3cm piece of fresh ginger, peeled and grated

100g breadcrumbs

2 tablespoons fish sauce

1 tablespoon soy sauce

freshly ground black pepper

sesame oil, for brushing

Beat the egg in a large bowl. Add all the other ingredients except the sesame oil and mix with your hands until well combined. You can blitz this in a food processor, but don't over-process – you want to keep some texture and bite.

Heat a small frying pan over a high heat. Break off a small amount of the mixture, flatten between your fingers and fry until cooked. Taste to check the seasoning and add more if necessary. Form the mixture into 18 small balls each about 4cm in diameter, packing each one firmly. Chill the balls for 15 minutes, and meanwhile bring a pan of water to the boil.

Line the bottom of a bamboo steamer with some baking parchment, or a banana leaf if you're feeling fancy … then brush the balls with sesame oil and lay them in the steamer. Steam on a high heat for 15 minutes, or until they are cooked through. You may have to steam the balls in two batches – don't overcrowd your steamer.

Serve the balls with Pickled Carrot & Daikon (page 148) and a bowl of soy sauce with sliced red chilli added, for dipping.

Serves
4

Baa Baa Balls

I was born on a British air force base in Cyprus, in the middle of the war in 1974.
This must have been where I developed my passion for Greek flavours, despite leaving before
I was a year old. Salty feta, with full-flavoured lamb and fresh mint is a classic combination
and will work just as well on a stuffed leg of lamb as it does here.

2 tablespoons olive oil

½ an onion, finely chopped

3 garlic cloves, crushed

1 large free-range egg

75g feta cheese, crumbled

500g lamb shoulder, minced

100g breadcrumbs

**2 tablespoons finely chopped
mint leaves**

1 teaspoon dried mixed herbs

1 teaspoon dried mint

½ teaspoon salt

1 tablespoon ground cumin

50ml double cream

**finely grated zest and juice
of 1 lime**

Preheat the oven to 220°C (425°F), Gas Mark 7 and line a large baking tray
with non-stick baking parchment.

Heat the oil in a large heavy-based pan. Add the onion and cook on a low
heat for 2 minutes. Add the garlic and cook for another 5 minutes, or until
the onion is soft and translucent.

Beat the egg in a large bowl. Add the feta, minced lamb, breadcrumbs, fresh
and dried herbs, salt, cumin, cream and lime zest and juice and mix with
your hands until well combined.

Heat a small frying pan over a high heat. Break off a small amount of the
mixture, flatten between your fingers and fry until cooked. Taste to check
the seasoning and add more if necessary. Form the mixture into 16 balls
each 5cm in diameter, packing each one firmly, and place them on the
prepared baking tray.

Bake for 18–20 minutes, turning the tray halfway through – the balls should
begin to brown on the top. Keep an eye on them to make sure that they
don't get burnt underneath.

Simply serve these straight from the oven with a dipping sauce of Cumin
Soured Cream (see page 111) or Spicy Lime Yoghurt (see page 113).

Serves
4–6

Ballymaloe Spicy Indian Meatballs

I had an amazing grandma. I called her GM cause she was a food loving, white wine drinking, Benson & Hedges-smoking, fashionable grandma. She called herself Ann because she didn't like her name, Emily. I quite like the name Emily. Still, 'Grandma' seemed too old and dusty, so GM she became. When she went to the smoking room in the sky, she left me a few thousand. I could have cleared the credit card debt but that didn't feel right. I wanted to do something good, something beneficial, to learn. It was to be the greatest gift, to learn how to cook. Then a friend mentioned Ballymaloe (cheers, Mo). If you like food, want to immerse yourself in growing, cooking and eating it for three months, then Ballymaloe is for you. Set on an organic farm near Cork, Ireland, it is a magical place to lay some culinary foundations, fish, butcher and forage. If you like Guinness, that's a bonus. If you like Beamish, better still. Ballymaloe. It's got a 'ball' in its name and it's run by the inspirational Darina Allen, who has kindly let me have her meatball recipe.

4 green cardamom pods

1½ teaspoons coriander seeds

1 clove

450g minced shoulder of lamb or beef

¼–½ teaspoon chilli powder

2–3 small garlic cloves, mashed

1 free-range egg

salt and freshly ground black pepper

Remove the seeds from the cardamom pods, discarding the husks. Grind the seeds in a pestle and mortar with the coriander and clove, then put into a bowl with the minced lamb, chilli powder, egg and mashed garlic and mix well. Season with salt and freshly ground black pepper.

Heat a small frying pan over a high heat. Break off a small amount of the mixture, flatten between your fingers and fry until cooked. Taste to check the seasoning and add more if necessary. Wet your hands with cold water, then form the mixture into 30–36 little meatballs each about 4cm in diameter.

Cover and chill until required, or cook immediately either on a barbecue or over a medium heat in a barely oiled frying pan. They will take a couple of minutes on each side.

Provide cocktail sticks or thread the cooked balls on to satay sticks, and serve with Darina's Pomegranate Seed & Coriander Raita (see page 121).

Lamb, Rosemary & Garlic Meatballs

Lamb, rosemary and garlic ... it's a classic combination and now it's in ball form.
Rosemary is such a hardy herb. Often it's used as a decorative plant, and I have, on the odd
occasion, been known to do a bit of neighbourly 'driveway foraging' for an emergency sprig ...

2 tablespoons olive oil

1 large onion, finely diced

4 garlic cloves, crushed

1 large free-range egg

500g lamb shoulder, minced

100g breadcrumbs

**2 tablespoons finely chopped
rosemary**

**2 tablespoons finely chopped
flat-leaf parsley**

2 teaspoons wholegrain mustard

zest of 1 lemon

**1 tablespoon freshly squeezed
lemon juice**

1 teaspoon salt

freshly ground black pepper

Preheat the oven to 220°C (425°F), Gas Mark 7 and line a baking tray with
non-stick baking parchment.

Heat the oil in a large heavy-based pan. Add the onions and cook on a low
heat for 2 minutes. Add the garlic and continue to cook on a low heat for
3 more minutes, or until the onion is translucent. Remove from the heat
and allow to cool.

Beat the egg in a large mixing bowl, then add the rest of the ingredients
and mix with your hands until well combined.

Heat a small frying pan over a high heat. Break off a small amount of the
mixture, flatten between your fingers and fry until cooked. Taste to check
the seasoning and add more if necessary. Form the mixture into 16 balls
each balls 5cm in diameter, packing each one firmly, and place them on
the prepared baking tray.

Bake for 15–18 minutes, turning the tray halfway through – the balls
should begin to brown on the top. Keep an eye on them to make sure that
the balls don't get burnt underneath.

I like to serve these Pudding Bowler style (see page 132) with Red Wine Gravy
(see page 90), and Honey-roasted Vegetables (see page 151).

Serves
4–6

Lamb, Goat's Cheese & Caramelized Onion Balls

We were asked to bring our balls to the Imperial Arms pub on the King's Road in May to do a pop-up residency. As it was spring, I thought we had better do a seasonal ball with lamb as the star. Lamb has such a great flavour, complementing the salty sweetness of the goat's cheese and onions.

1 large free-range egg

120g Caramelized Red Onions, chopped (see page 154)

2 garlic cloves, crushed

500g minced lamb shoulder

100g goat's cheese, crumbled

100ml milk

150g breadcrumbs

1 tablespoon finely chopped flat-leaf parsley

3 tablespoons finely chopped basil

1 teaspoon salt

¼ teaspoon freshly ground black pepper

Preheat the oven to 220°C (425°F), Gas Mark 7 and line a large baking tray with non-stick baking parchment.

Beat the egg into a large bowl. Add all the other ingredients and mix with your hands until well combined.

Heat a small frying pan over a high heat. Break off a small amount of the mixture, flatten between your fingers and fry until cooked. Taste to check the seasoning and add more if necessary. Form the mixture into 18 meatballs about 5cm in diameter, packing each one firmly, and place them on the prepared baking tray.

Bake for 18–20 minutes, turning the tray halfway through – the balls should begin to brown on the top. Keep an eye on them to make sure that they don't get burnt underneath.

Serve with Citrus Couscous (see page 147) and Honey-roasted Vegetables (see page 151). Any leftovers are just as nice cold for a super-charged packed lunch that will make your colleagues green with envy.

Serves
6

Ball Games – Game Balls

Occasionally I am lucky enough to be given a pheasant or a partridge, and I've come up with this recipe as a result. I've been getting into butchery, and I prefer to take the breasts from the birds without plucking them first. Otherwise it's a bit messy plucking a whole bird in our flat without the neighbours thinking a lunatic is on the loose. Your butcher can easily do it for you.

100g dried William pears

2 free-range eggs

100g dried breadcrumbs

500g pheasant breast meat, minced

250g unsmoked streaky bacon, minced

175ml double cream

2 tablespoons chopped flat-leaf parsley

1 garlic clove, crushed

1 teaspoon salt

freshly ground black pepper

Soak the dried pears in warm water for 15 minutes, then drain and finely chop.

Preheat the oven to 220°C (425°F), Gas Mark 7 and line 2 baking trays with non-stick baking parchment.

Lightly whisk the eggs in a large mixing bowl. In a separate bowl, mix together the chopped pears and breadcrumbs (these will stop the chopped pears sticking together). Add the pear and breadcrumb mix to the eggs, then stir in the minced pheasant and bacon, cream, parsley, garlic and salt. The mixture will initially seem very wet and will remain sticky – just keep mixing (using your hands is easiest) and you will find that the breadcrumbs will absorb the cream.

Heat a small frying pan over a high heat. Break off a small amount of the mixture, flatten between your fingers and fry until cooked. Taste to check the seasoning and add pepper and more salt if necessary.

Form the mixture into about 20–24 balls each 5cm in diameter, packing each one firmly, and place them on the prepared baking trays.

Bake for 15–20 minutes, turning the trays round halfway through – the balls should begin to brown on the top. Keep an eye on them to make sure that they don't get burnt underneath.

Nice served with Wild Mushroom Sauce (see page 92), mashed potatoes and sautéd Savoy cabbage.

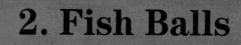

2. Fish Balls

Serves
4–6

Wasabi Salmon & Sesame Seed Balls

Wasabi is a Japanese root, from the same family as horseradish. When I first saw it I was surprised
to find that it isn't green, as the dye in many shop-bought varieties may lead you to believe.
I love the hit you get from having slightly too much wasabi; when it connects with the roof of
your mouth – eye watering, brain tingling, nasal passage-cleansingly great. I have increased
my tolerance over time, taking the pain along the way. I love it with salmon, so I had to use
it in this recipe. Be careful not to overcook the salmon otherwise it will dry out.

500g skinless salmon fillet

1 medium free-range egg

3 spring onions, thinly sliced

1 tablespoon chopped pickled ginger

1 teaspoon wasabi powder

2 tablespoons chopped coriander

**1 tablespoon freshly-squeezed
lemon juice**

1 tablespoon soy sauce or tamari

100g breadcrumbs

1 teaspoon salt

freshly ground black pepper

**3 tablespoons black sesame seeds,
toasted**

**3 tablespoons white sesame seeds,
toasted**

Preheat the oven to 220°C (425°F), Gas Mark 7 and line a large baking
tray with non-stick baking parchment.

Cut the salmon into 2cm cubes and place in the freezer for 20 minutes.
Once chilled, pulse in a food processor. Don't over-process, as you want
to retain some pieces of fish for texture.

Beat the egg in a large mixing bowl. Add the spring onions, pickled ginger,
wasabi powder, coriander, lemon juice, soy sauce, breadcrumbs, salt and
a sprinkling of pepper.

Heat a small frying pan over a high heat. Break off a small amount of the
mixture, flatten between your fingers and fry until cooked. Taste to check
the seasoning and add more lemon, ginger or wasabi powder if necessary.

Mix the two types of sesame seeds together and spread out on a plate.
Form the salmon mixture into 12–16 balls each about 5cm in diameter,
packing each one firmly. Roll the balls in the sesame seed mix and place
them on the prepared baking tray.

Bake for 10 minutes, turning the tray halfway through – the balls should
begin to brown on the top. Keep an eye on them to make sure that they
don't get burnt underneath.

Serve with Citrus Ponzu dipping sauce (see page 113).

Serves
4

Prawn Balls

Depending on who you are feeding, you can make a few variations to these balls. I love them with the pork added for an extra level of flavour and juiciness, but they are super tasty just made with prawns if you have a 'I don't eat meat but I do eat fish/shellfish' guest for dinner.

350g cooked prawns, deveined and washed (250g if combining with meat)

100g pork shoulder/chicken thighs, minced (optional)

1 free-range egg, beaten

2 tablespoon cornflour

50g Japanese panko breadcrumbs

2 spring onions or 2 shallots, finely chopped

2 garlic cloves, crushed

1 teaspoon sesame oil

2 teaspoons rice wine vinegar

1 tablespoon fish sauce

1 x 3cm piece of fresh ginger, peeled and grated

¼ teaspoon freshly ground black pepper

salt to taste

Japanese panko breadcrumbs, for coating (optional)

sunflower oil for frying

Drain the prawns and pat dry, then blitz them briefly in a food processor so that they are roughly chopped. Add the minced pork or chicken (if using), egg, cornflour and breadcrumbs and blitz again, so that everything comes together.

Turn the mixture out into a large bowl, add the rest of the ingredients apart from the coating crumbs and mix with your hands to combine. The mixture will be on the wet side but will firm up when chilled; however, if it seems too wet, add some more panko. Chill the mixture in the fridge for at least 30 minutes.

When you are ready to cook, wet your hands and form the mixture into 16 balls each about 4cm in diameter. At this stage, if you like, you can roll the balls in more of the panko breadcrumbs to give them a crisp, crunchy outside when fried.

Pour about 3cm of oil into a deep frying pan on a medium high heat. When the oil is hot and begins to shimmer, cook the balls in batches for 6 minutes, turning them after 2–3 minutes and heating the oil up again between batches. The balls should be golden brown and cooked through. Drain on kitchen paper before serving.

These balls are versatile. They're great on their own, with Cherry Tomato & Chilli Jam (see page 108) or Nuoc Cham dipping sauce (see page 119). Or, go 'Balls on the Line' style and skewer them after cooking, or, for the complete meal, stir-fry some garlic and red chilli in oil, add some shiitake mushrooms, soy sauce, Chinese cooking wine and pak choi/greens, then drop in the cooked prawn balls, heat through and serve with steamed rice.

Preparation time **40** minutes, plus freezing and chilling Cooking time **8-10** minutes

Serves
4–6

Tuna & Ginger Balls

These balls are best eaten on the day of cooking. The meaty tuna can stand up to the flavours of ginger and spring onions. Try to get line-caught skipjack tuna if possible and don't overcook them ... in fact, if your oven packs in, just eat them raw.

500g fresh tuna steak

1 large free-range egg

3 spring onions, finely sliced

2 garlic cloves, crushed

1 x 4cm piece of fresh ginger, peeled and finely chopped

2 tablespoons finely chopped coriander

1 red chilli, seeds removed, finely chopped

1 tablespoon Dijon mustard

1 tablespoon soy sauce

zest and juice of 1 lime

100g breadcrumbs

1 teaspoon salt

½ teaspoon freshly ground black pepper

Preheat the oven to 220ºC (425ºF), Gas Mark 7 and line a large baking tray with non-stick baking parchment.

Cut the tuna into 2cm cubes and place it in the freezer for 20 minutes. Once chilled, pulse in a food processor. Be careful not to over-process, as you want to retain some pieces of fish for texture.

Beat the egg in a large mixing bowl. Add the tuna, spring onions, garlic, ginger, coriander, chilli, Dijon mustard, soy sauce, lime zest and juice, breadcrumbs, salt and pepper, then mix with your hands until well combined.

Heat a small frying pan over a high heat. Break off a small amount of the mixture, flatten between your fingers and fry until cooked. Taste to check the seasoning and add more if necessary. Cover the mixture and refrigerate for at least 30 minutes.

Form the mixture into 14–16 balls each about 5cm in diameter (wetting your hands will make the balls easier to shape). Place the balls on the prepared baking tray.

Bake for 10–12 minutes, turning the tray halfway through – the balls should begin to brown on the top. I don't like to overcook tuna, as it's OK to eat it a little pink in the middle, so take a look at the balls after 8 minutes and decide how well done you want them to be. They are also good pan-fried in olive oil until browned all over.

These balls are great served in mini brioche slider buns, with rocket leaves and garlic mayo (see Real Mayonnaise on page 115), or with a rice noodle salad with Pickled Carrot & Daikon (see page 148).

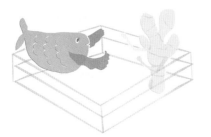

Serves
4–6

'Crab Ball-timore'

As a kid, heading to Whitsand Bay in Cornwall was a real treat. It was the local beach where Dad grew up, and his crabbing skills were Jedi-like. My brother and I would marvel as crabs were dislodged from their hiding places and put into our plastic buckets. Picking crabmeat without getting shell everywhere is tedious, but the sweet, soft meat is worth the work. The first references to 'crab cakes' appeared in cookbooks from Maryland, specifically Baltimore, USA in the early 1930s. These balls are inspired by those original recipes.

20g butter

3 spring onions, finely sliced, including green part

1 garlic clove, crushed

1 large free-range egg

2 tablespoons good mayonnaise

1 tablespoon chopped flat-leaf parsley

1 tablespoon chopped coriander

1 teaspoon English mustard powder

2 teaspoons Worcestershire sauce

1 tablespoon paprika

1 lime, zest finely grated, then the lime cut into wedges

1 teaspoon salt

a pinch of cayenne pepper

100g breadcrumbs

500g cooked crabmeat, white and brown

Japanese panko breadcrumbs, for coating (optional)

sunflower oil, for frying

Heat the butter in a large heavy-based pan. Add the spring onions and cook on a low heat for 2 minutes, then add the garlic and cook on a low heat for 3 more minutes, or until the white part of the onions is translucent and the green part soft. Remove from the heat and set aside to cool.

Beat the egg in a large mixing bowl, then add the mayonnaise, parsley, coriander, mustard powder, Worcestershire sauce, paprika, lime zest, salt and cayenne pepper. Finally, mix in the breadcrumbs, spring onion mixture, fold in the crabmeat, then mix with your hands until well combined.

Heat a small frying pan over a high heat. Break off a small amount of the mixture, flatten between your fingers and fry until cooked. Taste to check the seasoning and add more salt or cayenne if necessary. Form the mixture into 14–16 balls each 5cm in diameter, packing each one firmly. At this stage, if you like, you can roll the balls in panko breadcrumbs to give them a crisp, crunchy outside when fried.

To fry the crab balls, put 2 tablespoons of oil into a heavy-based pan. Heat the oil on a high heat until it shimmers, then cook the balls in batches for 6 minutes, turning them after 2–3 minutes and heating the oil up again between batches. The balls should be golden brown and cooked through. Drain on kitchen paper before serving.

Alternatively, you can bake the balls. Preheat the oven to 220°C (425°F), Gas Mark 7 and line a baking tray with non-stick baking parchment. Put the balls on the prepared tray and bake for 12 minutes, turning the tray halfway through – they should begin to brown on the top. Keep an eye on them to make sure that they don't get burnt underneath.

Try serving these balls each on top of a single baby gem lettuce leaf, with some Chipotle Mayonnaise (see page 115) and a wedge of lime or lemon, in front of a box set of *The Wire*.

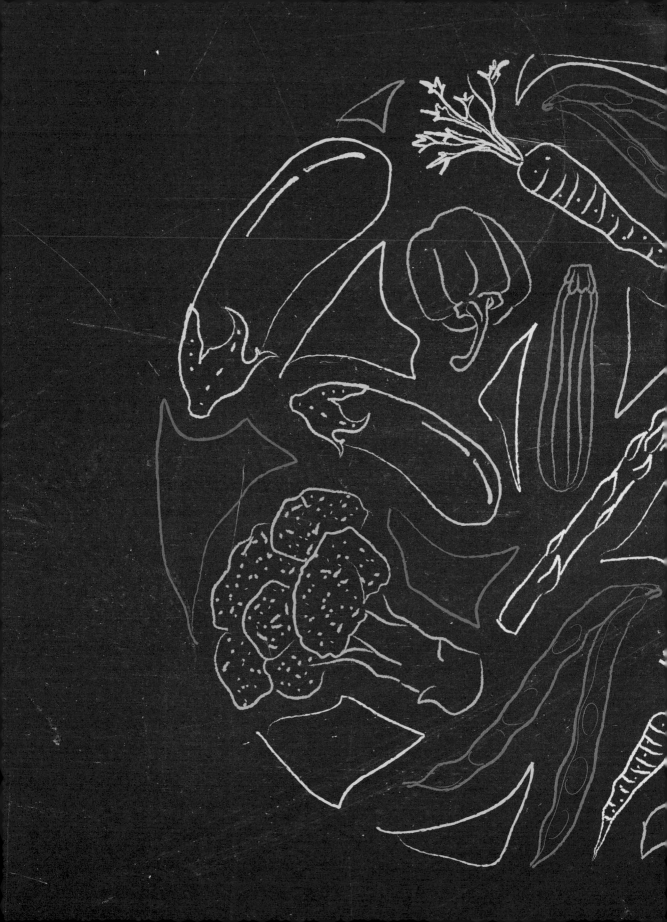

3. Veg Balls

Serves
4

Brown Rice & Red Lentil Balls

These super-healthy balls contain all you need to get a low-fat, nutritious hit of fibre,
protein and minerals. Try getting a few down the kids – all part of the fun after they
have shaped and baked them …

100g red lentils

olive oil

3 banana shallots, finely sliced

2 spring onions, finely sliced

1 garlic clove, crushed

120g pine nuts, toasted

**300g cooked brown rice, cooled
(weight 150g uncooked)**

2 teaspoons thyme, finely chopped

2 tablespoons basil, finely chopped

zest and juice of 1 lemon

1 large free-range egg

100g breadcrumbs

1 teaspoon salt

**½ teaspoon freshly ground
black pepper**

Preheat the oven to 220°C (425°F), Gas Mark 7 and line a large baking tray
with non-stick baking parchment.

Bring a pan of salted water to the boil. Add the lentils, bring back to the
boil and skim off the white foamy starch which will rise to the surface.
Cook for 5 minutes, or until the lentils are soft but haven't started to
disintegrate. Drain in a sieve and leave to cool.

Meanwhile, heat a little olive oil in a frying pan and add the shallots and
the white part of the spring onions. Stir-fry over a medium heat for
2 minutes, then add the garlic and cook until the onions are translucent.

Place the toasted pine nuts in a clean tea towel and bash them with the
back of a wooden spoon to break them (don't go too mad, though, as you
want to retain a few lumps for texture).

Beat the egg in a large bowl, then add all the other ingredients and mix
with your hands until well combined. Form the mixture into 16 balls each
5cm in diameter, packing each one firmly, and place them on the prepared
baking tray.

Bake the balls for 15–20 minutes, turning the tray round halfway through –
the balls should begin to brown on top. Keep an eye on them to make sure
they don't get burnt underneath.

Serve with Lowry & Baker's Chicory, Stilton, Pear & Pecan Salad (see
page 136), or with Simple Tomato Sauce (see page 99) and a green salad.

Serves
4–6

Balafel

This is my nod to the popular Middle Eastern dish falafel. Dried chickpeas are really easy to prepare and cook, the benefit being that you can control how soft to cook them, which is good if you want them to take a salad dressing or add texture. Always good to have a couple of tins tucked away though.

200g fresh spinach, washed

2 tablespoons olive oil

4 shallots, finely diced

2 garlic cloves, crushed

2 teaspoons cumin seeds

1 teaspoons coriander seeds

500g dried chickpeas, cooked
(see method on page 142)
or 2 x 400g tins chickpeas, drained

½ teaspoon dried chilli flakes

¼ teaspoon freshly ground nutmeg

2 teaspoons salt

¼ teaspoon black pepper

2 free-range eggs

200g ricotta cheese

150g breadcrumbs

1 tablespoon finely chopped
flat-leaf parsley

juice of 1 lemon

Preheat the oven to 220°C (425°F), Gas Mark 7 and line a large baking tray with non-stick baking parchment.

Put the washed, still wet spinach into a pan and add a splash of water. Cook over a high heat, turning regularly, until the spinach has wilted and softened. Squeeze it between two plates to get rid of excess liquid, then chop finely.

Put the olive oil into a heavy-based frying pan over a medium heat. Add the shallots, garlic and a sprinkling of salt and pepper. Stir-fry over a low heat for 6 minutes, or until the shallots are translucent, being careful not to burn the garlic (add a splash more oil if things start sticking), then add the spinach and stir frequently for a further 2 minutes. Leave to cool.

Heat a clean, heavy-based frying pan over a high heat and toast the cumin and coriander seeds for 2 minutes, moving them around in the pan so they don't burn, then grind them in a pestle and mortar.

Put the cooked chickpeas into a food processor with the cumin and coriander seeds, chilli flakes, nutmeg, salt and pepper, and pulse to get a rough paste. Make sure it isn't too fine, as you want a chunky texture.

Beat the eggs in a large bowl and stir in the ricotta. Add the breadcrumbs, spinach mixture, chickpea mixture, parsley and lemon juice and mix with your hands until well combined.

Heat a small frying pan over a high heat. Break off a small amount of the mixture, flatten between your fingers and fry until cooked. Taste to check the seasoning and add more if necessary.

With wet hands, form the mixture into 20 balls each about 5cm in diameter, packing each one firmly, then place the balls on the prepared baking tray. Bake for 15–20 minutes, turning the tray halfway through – the balls should begin to brown on the top. Make sure that they don't get burnt underneath.

These are great in a toasted pitta bread with some Cumin Soured Cream (see page 111) or Spicy Lime Yoghurt (see page 113).

Serves
3–4

Sweet Potato & Goat's Cheese Balls

The sweet potato is a favourite of mine for vegetarian dishes, as it can be baked whole, or fried to make crisps or chips, and has a great flavour. Kids love these colourful concoctions and they also make a quirky side dish to go with Sunday roasts.

600g sweet potatoes

200g spinach, washed

1 free-range egg

20g butter

1 garlic clove, crushed

1 tablespoon lemon juice

1 tablespoon double cream

100g fresh breadcrumbs

50g soft goat's cheese

1 teaspoon finely chopped rosemary

1 teaspoon salt

40g Parmesan cheese, finely grated, or a good vegetarian Parmesan-style cheese

40g Japanese panko breadcrumbs

freshly ground black pepper

Preheat the oven to 220ºC (425ºF), Gas Mark 7 and line a large baking tray with non-stick baking parchment.

Place the sweet potatoes on a baking tray and bake for 40 minutes, or until their flesh is soft and can be easily pierced with a knife. Remove from the oven, allow to cool to the touch, then peel.

Put the washed, still wet spinach into a large pan and add a splash of water. Cook over a high heat, turning the spinach over regularly, until it has wilted and softened. Squeeze it between two plates to get rid of any excess liquid, then chop it finely.

Mash the sweet potato in a large bowl with the egg, butter, garlic, lemon juice and cream. Add the spinach, fresh breadcrumbs, goat's cheese, rosemary, salt and a generous twist of pepper and mix thoroughly, using your hands. Place in the fridge for 30 minutes to an hour, to chill and set a little. Depending on the water content of the potatoes this can be quite a wet mixture, so add more breadcrumbs if you feel it won't hold its shape.

Mix the Parmesan and panko breadcrumbs together and put on a plate. Take the vegetable mixture out of the fridge and form it into 14–15 balls each about 5cm in diameter. Roll the balls in the Parmesan/panko mixture and place them on the prepared baking tray.

Bake the balls for 15–20 minutes, turning the tray around halfway through, until the balls begin to brown on top. Keep an eye on them to make sure that they don't get burnt underneath.

Great served with a baby leaf salad, toasted nuts and some crispy pancetta.

Serves
4

Courgette & Asparagus Balls

Grab the early season courgettes and combine them with the mid-season asparagus for a tasty veg ball option. It's important to remove as much liquid as possible from the grated courgettes to prevent sogginess and ball collapse – simply grab your cleanest tea towel and wring them out. Another thing to watch is when toasting the pine nuts – keep them moving around the pan so they don't burn. I am the king of distraction here. Whole pans of pine nuts have ended up in the bin because I have left them on the stove and forgotten about them. You have been warned...

4 small courgettes

2 teaspoons sea salt

25g pine nuts

2 free-range eggs

8 asparagus spears, trimmed and cut into 2mm rounds

2 garlic cloves, crushed

a large pinch of dried chilli flakes

100g fresh white breadcrumbs

6 tablespoons finely grated Parmesan cheese

200g Japanese panko breadcrumbs

Coarsely grate the courgettes into a bowl and sprinkle over 1 teaspoon of the salt. Set aside for 20 minutes to draw out some of the liquid, then squeeze the courgettes in a clean tea towel. This is important, because you want to remove as much liquid as you can in order to help the mixture combine and stick together.

Put the pine nuts into a dry frying pan and toast them over a medium heat, shaking the pan from time to time and making sure they don't burn. Remove the pan from the heat as soon as they start to turn a light brown colour and then tip them on to a board. When they've cooled down, crush them into small pieces.

Beat the eggs in a large bowl. Add the asparagus, grated courgettes, garlic, chilli flakes, white breadcrumbs, Parmesan, crushed pine nuts and another teaspoon of salt. Combine the mixture with a wooden spoon, then mix thoroughly using your hands, squeezing the mixture together as you go. The mixture will be fairly wet, so put it into the fridge for 30 minutes to chill and to allow the flavours to infuse.

Meanwhile, preheat the oven to 200°C (400°F), Gas Mark 6 and line a large baking tray with non-stick baking parchment.

Put the panko breadcrumbs into a shallow bowl. Form the courgette mixture into 12 balls each about 3–4cm in diameter, then roll them in the panko breadcrumbs and place them on the prepared baking tray. Bake in the oven for 15–20 minutes, turning the tray round halfway through – the balls should begin to brown on the top and be firm to touch. Keep an eye on them to make sure that they don't get burnt underneath.

Delicious served with Cheese Sauce (see page 103) and fresh pasta, with a poached egg on top.

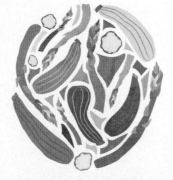

Balls 'n' Brews

When you are at a pop-up event you need a drink. A good bar takes a food market to the next level, and independent, artisan, craft brewers are on the rise. This is great news, as I am a big fan of hoppy pale ales and in the past the most readily available have been US imports. On trips to the US West Coast I've been surprised to see so many artisan breweries passionately sculpting ales from home-grown hops, so it's great to see there are now plenty of UK options, too. At the markets there have been regular ball-for-brew swaps. This cooperation has recently extended further, with the Camden Town Brewery hosting Street Feast, one of London's most high-profile night markets, bringing the food right into the brewers' backyard.

Andrew Cooper, accredited beer sommelier and founder of craft brewery The Wild Beer Co., is a big fan of pop-up event bars. It's a great way to get his brand out there to a core group of consumers who are passionate about what they eat and drink. Flavourful craft beers also lend themselves to pairing with food, with balls and brews having some great combinations. Here are Andrew's tips on which brews he thinks would best partner a few of my balls.

Beef & Chorizo Balls ~ Moor Illusion (Moor Beer Co.) A black IPA (India Pale Ale) is a great complement to these balls; earthy malt flavours work with the beef and juicy hops accentuate the spices in the chorizo.

Lamb, Rosemary & Garlic Meatballs ~ Modus Operandi (The Wild Beer Co.) Old English Ale aged for 90 days in oak barrels with wild yeast to produce a beer that is rich and fruity, with sweet cherries and tannins to complement the lamb.

Ballafel ~ Camden Pale (Camden Town Brewery) Punchy US hops throw out big aromas and flavours of grapefruit, orange and tropical fruit, which refresh the palate ready for the next bite.

Great Balls of Fire ~ Cannonball (Magic Rock Brewing Co.) Spices and hops are fabulous together, and this hoppy IPA has plenty of bitterness that nullifies the pungency of the spices, letting the hops and spices work together in a tongue-tingling taste sensation.

Crab Ball-timore ~ Fresh (The Wild Beer Co.) The freshest New World hops with stunning tropical fruit flavours and just a little bitterness so that it won't over-power the delicate crab, but is still incredibly moreish.

Smokin' Bacon Balls ~ Export India Porter (Kernel Brewery) Dark and roasty flavours are the perfect partner to the beef and bacon bombs, with the balancing hop presence in Kernel's masterpiece cleaning the palate of the delicious rich food.

Green Chilli Chicken ~ Bristol Hefe (Bristol Beer Factory) Light and spritzy with banana, citrus zest, grapefruit and spices that contrast and refresh the palate against the Thai chilli flavours.

Ball Games–Game Balls ~ Bliss (The Wild Beer Co.) A Belgian farmhouse-style beer brewed with a blend of spices, roasted apricots and a wild yeast; beautifully refreshing, wildly different.

4. Sauces & Dips

Red Wine Gravy

This one is going to come in handy whether you are serving it over a number of the
balls in this book, quality sausages and mash, or with the Sunday roast.

2 tablespoons olive oil

5 banana shallots, sliced

1 garlic clove, crushed

1 sprig of rosemary

30ml red wine vinegar

1 tablespoon redcurrant jelly

400ml red wine (Rioja works well)

400ml chicken or lamb stock

20g butter

salt and freshly ground black pepper

Heat the olive oil in a heavy-based pan over a medium heat. Add the shallots
and a couple of twists of salt and pepper, and stir for 5 minutes, or until the
shallots are soft and start to brown. Add the garlic and rosemary and cook for
a further 3 minutes, stirring occasionally to prevent it catching.

Stir in the red wine vinegar and redcurrant jelly, which should bubble up
and reduce fairly quickly to a syrupy consistency. Now add the red wine
and let it reduce by half before adding the stock. Simmer until the mixture
has reduced by two-thirds, then strain the sauce through a conical sieve,
removing the rosemary sprig.

Return the sauce to the pan, check the seasoning and add more salt if
required. Finally, stir in the butter to give the sauce a nice sheen.
Great served with Lamb, Rosemary & Garlic Meatballs (see page 60).

● ● ● ● ● ● ● ●

Chicken Stock

Fresh chicken stock is easy to make if you remember not to bin the Sunday roast leftovers.
Simply put a stockpot on before settling down in front of *The Antiques Roadshow*, or freeze
the carcass until a later date when you have a few more of them to make a bumper batch.
You can ask your butcher for chicken carcasses if you want to get your hands on some quickly.

3 chicken carcasses, raw or cooked

1 onion, sliced

1 carrot, sliced

1 celery stick, sliced

1 leek, sliced

a few sprigs of parsley

a sprig of thyme

1 bayleaf, torn

6 white peppercorns

Remove any excess fat from the chicken, then place all the ingredients in
a stockpot big enough to hold them. Fill the pot with enough water to just
cover the carcass, about 3 litres.

Bring to a simmer and skim off any fat and foam that appear on the surface.
Keep at a very low simmer for 3 hours, skimming regularly, then pass the
liquid through a fine sieve. To increase the flavour of the stock, reduce
it rapidly to half its original volume or until it tastes right to you. Set aside
to cool.

You can keep reducing the stock down, then freeze the concentrated stock
in ice cube trays – these can then be diluted for use in smaller batches.

Wild Mushroom Sauce

This is a rich sauce, but if you're not a rich person you can thin it with a little stock
or use single cream.

50g butter

2 tablespoons olive oil

6 banana shallots

**250g button mushrooms
or mushroom trimmings,
roughly chopped**

**1 head of garlic, cut in half
horizontally**

4 sprigs of thyme

250ml white wine

350ml chicken stock

350ml double cream

**200g mixed wild mushrooms,
cleaned**

**1 tablespoon freshly squeezed
lemon juice**

salt and freshly ground black pepper

Melt 25g of the butter with the oil in a heavy-based pan. Finely slice 3 of
the shallots and add them to the pan, along with the button mushrooms/
mushroom trimmings, garlic, thyme and salt. Cook gently for 15–20 minutes,
stirring occasionally to prevent the mixture catching, until you have a soft,
mushy, caramelized mixture.

Add the wine and let it simmer until reduced by two-thirds to a syrupy
consistency. Add the chicken stock and simmer until reduced by half, then
add the cream. Keep simmering, letting the sauce reduce by half again so
that you get a nice thick consistency that coats the back of a spoon. Season
to taste, then strain the sauce through a conical sieve, crushing and pushing
all the tasty bits through with the back of a spoon or ladle.

Finely chop the remaining 3 shallots. Melt the remaining butter in a large
deep-sided frying pan until it foams, then add the shallots, stirring for
5 minutes until they start to soften.

Add the wild mushrooms and cook slowly until the liquid they give off
has evaporated. Add half the lemon juice and stir.

Stir in your strained sauce and let it reheat. Once simmering, add the
last of the lemon juice, then check the seasoning and serve.

Barbecue Sauce

I use this as the base for the Honey & Garlic Sticky Ball Sauce (see page 96).
However, it's a versatile little number that can also be used for marinating chicken, pork
and sausages prior to barbecuing, basting meat just before it comes off the coals, or just as a
dipping sauce. It gets even better after a few days mingling, once the flavours have chatted to
one another. If you want a thinner sauce without the lumps of tomato, purée it in a liquidizer.

2 tablespoons olive oil

1 small onion, very finely chopped

1 garlic clove, crushed

1 tablespoon tomato purée

1 x 400g tin of chopped tomatoes

3 tablespoons cider vinegar

2 tablespoons tomato ketchup

2 tablespoons Worcestershire sauce

2 tablespoons pure honey

1 tablespoon Dijon mustard

1 tablespoon dark brown sugar

1 teaspoon sweet smoked paprika

½ teaspoon Tabasco

juice of 1 lemon

salt and freshly ground black pepper

Heat the oil in a heavy-based saucepan. Add the onion and cook on a low heat for 2 minutes. Add the garlic and cook for another 3 minutes, or until the onion is soft and translucent, then add the tomato purée and stir for 3 minutes.

Now add all the other ingredients apart from the salt and pepper, and bring to the boil. Simmer for 15 minutes.

Season to taste and if possible leave to rest for an hour before using. It's even better if left for a day before using in the Sticky Ball Sauce, as this allows time for the flavours to really develop.

Honey & Garlic Sticky Ball Sauce

This sauce uses my homemade Barbecue Sauce as a base (see page 95).
Honey and garlic may, at first, seem like an unlikely combination,
but go with it – it works really well.

1 tablespoon olive oil

5 garlic cloves, crushed

75ml mild clear honey

1 tablespoon soy sauce

**250ml Barbecue Sauce
(see page 95), or your favourite
ready-made version**

100ml tomato passata

Heat the olive oil in a medium-sized pan over a medium heat. Add the garlic and cook over a low heat for 2 minutes, then add the rest of the ingredients and bring to a simmer. Cook, stirring frequently, for a further 3 minutes.

Use it in Sticky Balls (see page 33) or as a dip.

Chipotle Tomato Sauce

The chipotle chilli is a smoke-dried jalapeño which is commonly used in Mexican cooking.
It is great added to mayonnaise or used in a barbecue marinade, and gives this tomato sauce
a rich smoky flavour, perfect for Burritos (see page 22).

3 tablespoons extra virgin olive oil

3 red onions, thinly sliced

2 medium red chillies, seeds removed, chopped

2 garlic cloves, crushed

3 tablespoons finely chopped coriander stalks

2 tablespoons Bowler's Dry Spice Blend (see page 122)

1 tablespoon tomato purée

2 x 400g tins of Italian/quality chopped tomatoes

400ml Chicken Stock (see page 90)

25g soft light brown sugar

2 tablespoons Chipotles in Adobo (available at www.coolchile.co.uk)

juice of 1–2 limes

salt and freshly ground black pepper

Heat the olive oil in a wide deep pan. Add the onions and cook gently with a lid on the pan for 10 minutes, or until very soft but not browned. At this stage, I would always add a few pinches of salt and grinds of pepper so the onions are seasoned from the start, meaning that you don't have to add so much later in the recipe.

Add the chillies, garlic, coriander and Bowler's Dry Spice Blend and stir for 5 minutes, or until the chillies have started to soften, making sure the mixture doesn't catch on the bottom of the pan and burn. Add the tomato purée and cook for 3 minutes, again stirring so that it doesn't catch. Add the tinned tomatoes, chicken stock and a few pinches of salt, bring to the boil, then simmer for 20 minutes, stirring occasionally to avoid sticking.

Add three-quarters of the sugar, followed by 2 teaspoons of salt and the Chipotles in Adobo. Stir and simmer for another 30 minutes, then taste. Add more sugar if necessary, as the sweetness can vary depending on the flavour of the tomatoes. Add the lime juice at the end, to keep the freshness. You should now have a thick, rich smoky sauce. Adjust the seasoning, adding more salt or chillies as necessary.

Simple Tomato Sauce

I'm a big fan of all things spicy, but some occasions call for toning it down. Not a lot goes with a meatball better than pasta, Parmesan and a thick, slow-cooked tomato sauce, great for kids and adults alike. Of course, if you can't face life without a little heat, just drop in a chilli.

2 tablespoons olive oil

3 garlic cloves, halved

1 onion, finely chopped

3 x 400g cans San Marzano tomatoes or good quality Italian plum tomatoes, drained with their juice reserved

½ teaspoon dried oregano

sugar, to taste

salt and freshly ground black pepper

Heat the oil in a heavy-based saucepan over a medium heat. Add the garlic and cook for 2 minutes, or until it begins to turn golden, then add the onion and a pinch of salt. Turn down the heat and cook gently for 3 minutes.

Add the tomatoes and oregano and cook slowly. Break up the tomatoes with a wooden spoon after a couple of minutes. If it looks like it's sticking, add a little of the tomato juice.

Slowly cook this out for 1 hour, uncovered, then season to taste with salt, pepper and a pinch or two of sugar if the tomatoes aren't singing with sweetness by themselves. You can serve the sauce before the hour is up if you are short of time, but it won't be as thick or rich.

Serve with any number of meatballs … or as it is with some fresh pasta.

Spiced Red Onion & Tomato Sauce

When I'm asked what gives this sauce its flavour, I simply say, 'I just get all the spices you can buy whole, toast them, grind them and put them into the sauce.' Although this is a slight exaggeration, it's pretty much the case. Be sure to take your time with this sauce, making sure the onions cook down slowly, then let the sauce reduce for a rich flavour.

3 tablespoons extra virgin olive oil

3 onions, thinly sliced

1 x 5cm piece of fresh root ginger, peeled and finely chopped

3 medium red chillies, seeds removed, finely sliced

2 garlic cloves, crushed

3 tablespoons finely chopped coriander stalks

2 tablespoons Bowler's Dry Spice Blend (see page 122)

1 tablespoon tomato purée

2 x 400g tins of Italian/quality chopped tomatoes

400ml Chicken Stock (see page 90)

25g soft light brown sugar

3 tablespoons soy sauce

75g dried cranberries or sultanas/ raisins

juice of 1 lime

salt and freshly ground black pepper

Heat the olive oil in a large, deep pan over a low-medium heat. Add the onions, stir, then cover the pan and leave to cook gently for 10 minutes, or until very soft, but not browned. At this stage, I would always add a few pinches of salt and several grinds of pepper so that the onions are seasoned from the start, meaning that you won't have to add so much later in the recipe.

Add the ginger, chillies, garlic, coriander stalks and Bowler's Dry Spice Blend and stir for 4 minutes, or until the chillies start to soften, making sure nothing catches on the base of the pan and burns. Then stir in the tomato purée and cook for 3 minutes, stirring all the time.

Add the chopped tomatoes, chicken stock and a few pinches of salt and bring to the boil, then simmer for 30 minutes, stirring occasionally to prevent the sauce from sticking.

Add three-quarters of the sugar, the soy sauce and the dried fruit. Stir and simmer for a further 15 minutes, then taste. The sweetness of the sauce can vary depending on the flavour of the tomatoes, so add more sugar or soy sauce if necessary. Taste again and add some or all of the lime juice. You should now have a thick, rich sauce that has a deep, sweet and sour flavour with warmth from the chillies and spices.

Best served with Great Balls of Fire (see page 34).

Crispy Cream

Crispy Cream, after my aforementioned mate Crispin who went to Sweden for a lady, is my take on the Swedish cream sauce that goes particularly well with the Björn Balls (see page 46). It uses a basic roux – a thickening agent made by combining flour and butter. You can make a batch and store it in the fridge for up to 2 weeks, so it's on hand for dropping into gravies and sauces.

2 tablespoons butter

2 tablespoons plain flour

juice of 1 lemon

600ml beef stock

1 tablespoon lingonberry jam, or cranberry jam

120ml double cream, or soured cream

salt and freshly ground black pepper

Heat the butter in a large heavy-based pan, then add the flour and stir for 2 minutes to cook out the raw flour flavour, making a roux. Turn up the heat and add the lemon juice and the stock gradually, stirring constantly as you go, so the roux gets incorporated. Stir in the jam, which will make the sauce go a creamy orange colour. Once the liquid reaches boiling point, turn the heat down and add the cream. Simmer the sauce for 20 minutes, uncovered, to reduce it until it thickens and will coat the back of a spoon.

Add the chilled Björn Balls to the sauce and cook with a lid on for 20 minutes, turning them until warmed through. If the sauce gets a little too thick, add more stock. Adjust the seasoning and serve.

● ● ● ● ● ● ● ●

Blue Cheese Sauce

Blue cheese loves beef so this cold dipping sauce can really come in handy. I love it with Ball Shiitake (see page 27), and it makes a great dressing for salads too.

1 small garlic clove, crushed

100ml mayonnaise

100ml soured cream

60g blue cheese, e.g. Cashel Blue, Stilton or Gorgonzola, crushed

1 tablespoon white wine vinegar

1 tablespoon chopped chives or green spring onion tops

salt and freshly ground black pepper

Put all the ingredients into a bowl and whisk until smooth.

Transfer to a jam jar and store in the fridge – it will keep for up to 4 days.

Cheese Sauce

This is a universal sauce that works in a lot of combinations, so do experiment with it. It's the perfect accompaniment to pasta, polenta and naked balls on a salad. I served this the very first time I got my balls out in public at a pop-up night, on top of Courgette & Asparagus Balls (see page 84).

60g butter

60g plain flour

600ml milk

400ml double cream

1 garlic clove, left unpeeled, squashed with the flat of a knife

1 bay leaf

2 teaspoons salt

70g Parmesan or Gruyère cheese, freshly grated

freshly ground black pepper

Heat the butter in a large heavy-based pan. Add all the flour and stir for a couple of minutes to cook out the raw flour flavour. Gently whisk in the milk, cream, garlic, bay leaf and salt. Stir continuously, until the liquid comes up to boiling point and starts to thicken. Simmer on the lowest heat setting for 5 minutes, continuing to stir.

Stir in the cheese until it has melted, and add a good few turns of black pepper. Check the seasoning, and fans of cheese had better check the cheesiness ... add a little more if the mood takes you.

Take the pan off the heat and fish out the garlic and bay leaf. If you are not serving immediately, cover the surface with clingfilm so that a skin doesn't form. Fresh herbs such as parsley and thyme can also be added to this sauce.

Guacamole

Guacamole is a key element of the Luardos burrito that's also perfect in other combinations. It's straight out of a Mexican cookery school in Oaxaca, where all the crushing and mixing was done with a pestle and mortar. As we pair it up with our balls, we like to keep it chunky, so don't go too mad with the processor/fork/pestle. It's absolutely crucial the avocados are ones with a rich, creamy texture. If they're not, it's probably not worth making.

4 ripe Hass avocados

1 tablespoon extra virgin olive oil

3 tablespoons lime juice

½ a garlic clove, crushed

¼ of a jalapeño chilli, finely chopped

1 tablespoon chopped coriander

½ a large red onion, finely chopped

1 ripe tomato, deseeded and finely chopped

sea salt and freshly ground pepper

Scoop the avocado flesh into a bowl and roughly mash. Mix in the remaining ingredients and season with salt and pepper to taste.

I lather this in Simon's Burritos (see page 22), but it's also amazing as a dip with Smokin' Bacon Balls (see page 41) and alongside our salads.

Tomato Salsa aka Pico de Gallo

Here's a tomato salsa recipe from our friends Luardos. It is a very simple fresh salsa and is absolutely crucial in the making of a good Burrito (see page 22). It's important to get the balance between sweet (sugar) and sour (lime) right. This will depend slightly on the ripeness of the tomatoes, so a little adjustment is sometimes required.

6 ripe tomatoes, cored, deseeded and finely diced

½ a Spanish onion, finely diced

½ a red onion, finely diced

1 tablespoon chopped coriander

1 tablespoon extra virgin olive oil

1 bird's-eye chilli, finely sliced (optional)

a pinch of sea salt

3 tablespoons fresh lime juice

½ teaspoon caster sugar

Put all the ingredients into a bowl and mix well. Give it a taste and add a little more lime juice and/or sugar if required.

Cover and set aside for 30 minutes to let the flavours combine.

Cherry Tomato & Chilli Jam

I love chilli jam and eat it on all sorts of things. I put this with the balls I serve with the Coconut Curry Sauce (see page 117), as the sweetness really works with the spices. I also whizz whole chillies to add extra kick, but you can remove the seeds beforehand if you prefer. I always try a little bit of raw chilli before I cook with them – the heat can really vary from one chilli to another, so a taste helps to determine how much or how little, seeds or no seeds, to go with.

2 garlic cloves, chopped

2 red chillies, chopped

1 x 2.5cm piece of fresh ginger, grated

2 tablespoons fish sauce or soy sauce

1 teaspoon cumin seeds

2 teaspoons coriander seeds

400g cherry tomatoes, halved (or equivalent tin of regular chopped tomatoes)

100ml red wine vinegar

200g golden caster sugar

Place the garlic, chillies, ginger and fish sauce into a food processor and pulse to form a paste.

Heat a heavy-based non-stick frying pan over a medium heat until it begins to smoke, then add the cumin and coriander seeds. Toast them for about 3 minutes, or until they begin to brown, start to pop and give off a fragrant aroma. Remove them from the heat and grind them in a pestle and mortar.

Put the paste from the processor into a wide pan over a medium heat and add the tomatoes, vinegar, sugar and ground spices. Turn up the heat and bring the mixture to a boil, then turn the heat down and simmer for 30–45 minutes, stirring regularly until it thickens to a jam-like consistency. When you draw a spoon through the jam it should leave a line for a second. It will thicken up a little more when it cools, but definitely hold your nerve and don't pull the pan off the heat early.

Transfer the mixture into jam jars, put the lids on and leave to cool. I sterilize jars by putting them into an oven heated to 150°C (300°F), Gas Mark 2 for 15 minutes and soaking the lids in boiling water for 5 minutes.

Serve with Green Chilli Chicken Balls (see page 52), as a dip for Balls on the Line (see page 24), or even with a cheese board.

Cumin Soured Cream

I use this on Great Balls of Fire, as it rounds the dish off well. It can make a tasty dip for raw veg and crisps, too. For the best flavour I always recommend toasting whole cumin seeds and grinding them, but the ready-ground spice short-cut works too.

1 teaspoon cumin seeds

150ml soured cream

100ml Greek-style yoghurt

a pinch of cayenne pepper

1 small garlic clove, crushed (optional)

salt

Heat a heavy-based non-stick frying pan over a medium heat until it begins to smoke. Add the cumin seeds, shaking the pan constantly until they give off a nice aroma and begin to pop. Remove them from the heat, let them cool down a little, then grind them to a powder using a pestle and mortar.

Put the soured cream, yoghurt, cayenne, and garlic (if using) into a bowl, stir and add the ground cumin seeds and salt to taste.

● ● ● ● ● ● ● ●

Garam Masala

Garam masala is a spice blend that is used a lot in Indian cooking. 'Garam' means hot and 'masala' means spice. It's often added to dishes towards the end of cooking, and it's wise to add it little by little, as it can overpower dishes quite easily. You can buy a ready-made mix if you're pressed for time. I use it to spice the Green Chilli Chicken Balls (see page 52).

seeds from 30 green cardamom pods, husks removed

15 cloves

seeds from 5 black cardamom pods, husks removed

4 pieces of mace

4 x 2.5cm sticks of cinnamon

5 tablespoons cumin seeds

2 tablespoons coriander seeds

1 teaspoon black peppercorns

Put a dry frying pan over a medium heat and add all the spices, stirring continually to keep the seeds moving. After 1–2 minutes there will be an aroma as the seeds begin to release their oils. Once this happens, remove the pan from the heat, pour the spices on to a plate and leave them to cool.

If you're using an electric grinder or processor, wait until the spices are cool to the touch, then grind. Alternatively use a pestle and mortar and grind to a fine powder by hand.

Allow to cool completely, then store in an airtight container. As long as the container is tightly closed after each use, the garam masala should last a long time. I like to make it fresh every 2 months.

Spicy Lime Yoghurt

This tasty sauce and dip is cooling yet warming at the same time. You can add chopped
mint leaves instead of the coriander, depending on what you might want to serve it with.
I like things spicy, so I'd advise adding half the lime juice and half the Tabasco to start with,
then adding the remainder to taste.

250ml Greek-style yoghurt

**2 tablespoons finely chopped
coriander leaves**

finely grated zest and juice of 1 lime

1 teaspoon Tabasco sauce

1 tablespoon extra virgin olive oil

Simply mix the yoghurt and coriander together in a bowl with half the
lime juice and Tabasco. Taste, add more lime and Tabasco if necessary,
then beat in the oil.

Cover and refrigerate until ready to use. Would be nice with Baa Baa Balls
(see page 56) or Balafel (see page 81).

Citrus Ponzu

Ponzu is a Japanese sauce or dressing made by combining citrus juice and soy sauce.
The traditional citrus fruit used is called yuzu, but lime is much easier to find so I'm using that.

juice of 1 lime

**1 tablespoon Japanese rice
wine vinegar**

2 tablespoons light soy sauce

1 teaspoon golden caster sugar

1 teaspoon sesame oil

1 teaspoon mirin (optional)

zest of 1 lime

Put all the ingredients into a bowl and whisk until the sugar has dissolved.

This sauce gets better if it is refrigerated for a few hours or overnight,
to allow the flavours to mingle.

To make a dressing for salads, simply whisk the above sauce with some
sesame oil … hey, why not go mad and throw some sesame seeds in
there too …

Chipotle Mayonnaise

This smoky-tasting mayo is great to use as a dip for chips, chicken or fish, to spread on a sandwich or a burger, or to pimp a bacon and egg butty.

1 chipotle chilli

150ml Real Mayonnaise (see below)

1 garlic clove, crushed

1 teaspoon adobe sauce

1 spring onion, green parts only, finely sliced

1 tablespoon fresh lime juice

sea salt flakes and freshly ground black pepper

Soak the chipotle chilli in warm water for 15 minutes, then chop it finely.

Put all the ingredients into a large bowl and whisk together.

● ● ● ● ● ● ● ●

Real Mayonnaise

You need to be able to make your own mayonnaise so that you can customize it with other ingredients and then lather it on to your baps, balls and burgers. When you've done it once, and seen how easy it is, there's no turning back. Just use a food processor. To save on wastage this recipe uses whole eggs; the whites help to stabilize the mixture. If you want a richer mayonnaise, add another egg yolk, increase the oil and adjust the other ingredients to taste. I use olive pomace oil because it's lighter than olive oil and less likely to overpower the mayonnaise with an olive taste, but you should experiment and mix oils together to achieve a taste you like.

2 free-range eggs

1 tablespoon Dijon mustard

350ml olive pomace oil, olive oil, sunflower oil, or a combination

1 tablespoon white wine vinegar, cider vinegar or lemon juice

freshly ground salt and black pepper

Put the eggs, mustard, salt and pepper into the bowl of a food processor and pulse briefly to combine.

With the motor running, drizzle the oil in, slowly to begin with and then faster, as the eggs and oil begin to emulsify. Once the mixture has thickened up, add the vinegar. Taste, and increase the mustard, vinegar, salt and pepper to your liking. At this stage you can also add other ingredients like some Confit Garlic (see page 155), coriander and other herbs, chillies and other spices.

Coconut Curry Sauce

This Thai-inspired sauce is delicious with Green Chilli Chicken Balls (see page 52), but also works with Great Balls of Fire (see page 34). Thai food has very distinctive flavours that work together and need to be balanced: sweet, sour, hot and salty. In this recipe sweetness comes from the palm sugar and the coconut milk, sourness from the limes, heat from the chillies and saltiness from the fish sauce – balance these to taste, and add the customary Thai basil and slivers of kaffir lime leaf for an authentic finish.

THE PASTE

1 tablespoon coriander seeds

1 tablespoon cumin seeds

10 fresh green Thai bird's-eye chillies, seeds removed, chopped

2 banana shallots, chopped

3 garlic cloves, roughly chopped

1 x 3cm piece of fresh ginger, or galangal if you can find it

3 medium lemongrass stems, tough ends and outer layer removed, chopped

3 kaffir lime leaves

3 tablespoons chopped coriander

1 teaspoon shrimp paste

1 teaspoon Thai fish sauce

½ teaspoon freshly ground black pepper

THE SAUCE

1 tablespoon groundnut or vegetable oil

1 tablespoon paste (see above)

400ml coconut milk

2 teaspoons palm sugar

1 tablespoon Thai fish sauce

juice of 1 lime

2 kaffir lime leaves or zest of 1 lime

1 tablespoon Thai basil, chopped into slivers

Heat a heavy-based non-stick frying pan over a medium heat until it begins to smoke. Add the coriander and cumin seeds, shaking the pan constantly until they give off a nice aroma and begin to pop. Once this happens, remove from the heat and pour them on to a plate to cool. When the spices are cool, grind them to a powder using a pestle and mortar.

Put the rest of the paste ingredients into a food processor, add the ground seeds and pulse to make a paste.

Heat the oil in a heavy-based pan over a medium heat. Add 1 tablespoon of the paste and cook for 2 minutes, then add the coconut milk, stir to combine, and bring to a simmer.

Add the palm sugar, fish sauce, lime juice and lime leaves. Taste, and balance the sweet, sour and salty with a little more palm sugar, lime and fish sauce if required. Simmer for 10 minutes, remove from the heat, stir in the Thai basil and serve.

Peanut Sauce

Satay with attitude – great for dipping Green Chilli Chicken Balls into (see page 52), spreading on a piece of leftover naan bread, or, once chilled, using as a dip for raw veg.

2 tablespoons vegetable oil

1 small red onion, finely chopped

1 small red chilli, seeds removed and chopped

1 garlic clove, crushed

150ml unsweetened coconut milk

3 tablespoons hot water

1 tablespoon dark soy sauce

4 tablespoons smooth peanut butter

4 tablespoons chopped roasted peanuts

1 tablespoon fresh lime juice

salt and freshly ground black pepper

Heat the oil in a medium pan. Add the onions and cook over a low heat for 2 minutes, then add the chilli and garlic and cook, stirring frequently, for a further 3 minutes, or until the onion is soft.

Add the coconut milk and bring to the boil. Turn off the heat, add the hot water and soy sauce, then whisk in the peanut butter. Stir in the chopped peanuts and lime juice, and season the sauce with salt and pepper to taste.

Keep in a sealed jar in the fridge for up to 3–4 days. When it is chilled the sauce will get thicker, so either use as a dip or soften it up in a pan over a low heat, adding a splash of water if necessary.

Nuoc Cham

This sauce is a staple in Vietnam. Primarily a dipping sauce for just about everything,
it balances the sweet, sour, salty and spicy elements that make Asian cooking so damn good
and gives a nice flavour to the pork balls used in Vietnamese Noodle Soup (see page 18).

125ml water

50g granulated sugar

**3 tablespoons freshly squeezed
lime juice**

1 tablespoon rice wine vinegar

2 small garlic cloves

**2 red Thai chillies, seeds removed
and finely chopped**

½ teaspoon salt

3 tablespoons fish sauce

Put the water, sugar, lime juice and vinegar into a bowl and stir to
dissolve the sugar. Taste to check the balance of sweet and sour, making
adjustments if necessary.

Combine the garlic, chillies and salt, using a pestle and mortar to create
a smooth paste.

Mix the garlic paste with the liquid in the bowl and add the fish sauce.
Stir and taste again, checking the balance of sour, sweet, salt and spice.

SAUCES & DIPS

Pomegranate Seed & Coriander Raita

Darina Allen's recipe for when you've over-spiced your balls – this refreshing raita will help cool you down. A perfect accompaniment to the Ballymaloe Spicy Indian Meatballs (see page 59).

a large pinch of cumin seeds

1 pomegranate

275ml natural yoghurt

2–3 tablespoons coarsely chopped coriander

salt and freshly ground pepper

Put the cumin seeds into a dry frying pan and roast over a high heat, shaking the pan frequently, for a minute, or until the seeds start to give off an aroma. Set aside to cool.

Split the pomegranate in half around the equator, then hold cut side down over a bowl and tap vigorously with the back of a wooden spoon – the seeds should dislodge and fall into the bowl.

Add the yoghurt, coriander and the freshly roasted cumin seeds, and season with salt and freshly ground pepper.

Serve with hot spicy dishes.

The Bowler's Dry Spice Blend

This is a great way to add some deep spice to your sauces and other cooking. It really pays to buy all these spices whole and toast them in a dry non-stick heavy-based pan. Once toasted, the spices can be ground in a pestle and mortar, coffee grinder or food processor. The flavour you get from whole spices is much more intense and fresh than that of their ready-ground brothers, which will lose flavour once they hit the packet and certainly once opened.

1 tablespoon fennel seeds

1 tablespoon coriander seeds

1 tablespoon cumin seeds

1 tablespoon fenugreek seeds

½ a star anise

1 whole cardamom pod

1 dried bay leaf

1 x 4cm stick of cinnamon, broken

¼ teaspoon ground nutmeg

1 tablespoon black or yellow mustard seeds

½ teaspoon nigella seeds

Heat a heavy-based non-stick frying pan over a medium heat until it starts to smoke.

Add all the ingredients to the dry pan except the mustard seeds and nigella seeds, and shake the pan every few seconds to keep the spices moving. After 1 minute add the mustard seeds and nigella seeds.

After a further minute there will be a nutty, fragrant aroma coming off the pan and the coriander seeds and fennel seeds will start to turn a red-brown colour. Once this happens and the seeds begin to pop, remove the pan from the heat and tip the spices on to a plate to cool down. (If you leave them in the pan they will continue to cook and will quickly burn.)

If using an electric grinder or processor, make sure the spices are cool to the touch before grinding in batches – if they are still hot they can give off a bit of moisture and stick to the sides of the machine. Alternatively use a pestle and mortar and grind the spices to a fine powder by hand.

Once ground, you can keep this spice mix in an airtight container for up to 4 weeks. Use in the Chipotle Tomato Sauce (see page 98), Spiced Red Onion & Tomato Sauce (see page 100) or try adding some to a meatball mixture or use to flavour couscous.

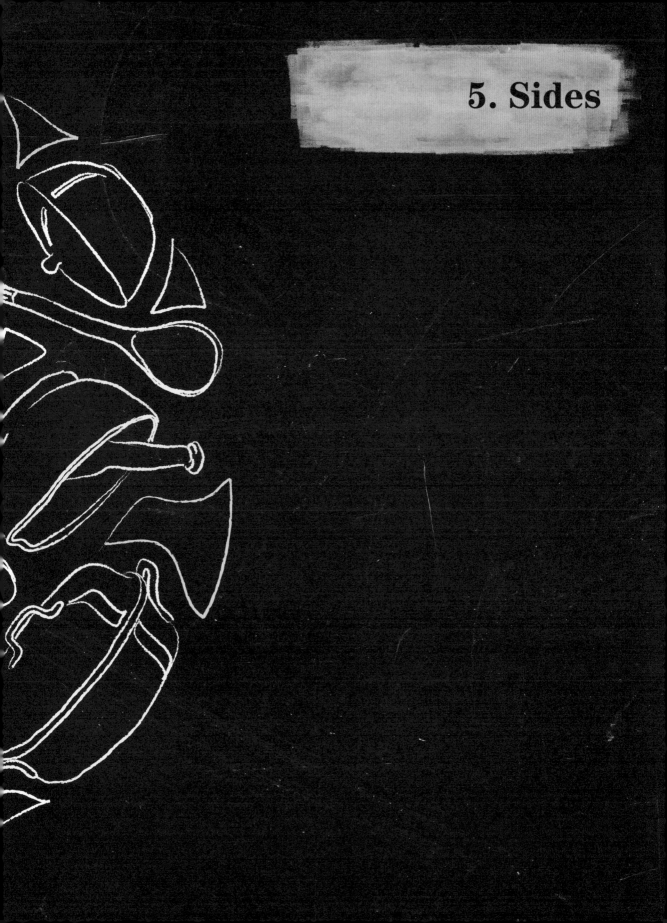

5. Sides

Cheesed, Charred & Herbed Polenta

Polenta is a great side for meatballs, as it sits perfectly under any sauce and mops up leftovers brilliantly. You can also pour it into a baking tray about 1cm thick, set it aside to cool, then slice it up and chargrill or fry it with a little olive oil.

1 litre water

1 teaspoon salt

175g coarse polenta

80g butter

75g Parmesan cheese, grated

freshly ground black or white pepper

Put the water and salt into a large pan and bring to a rolling boil. Use a measuring jug to pour the polenta into the water, whisking as you go. Continue to stir until it comes to a boil, burping bubbles up, then turn the heat down to low. Continue to cook it for up to an hour (40–45 minutes might be enough), stirring regularly.

If you make a big, double-quantity recipe batch, you can pour off half the polenta into a buttered baking tray at this stage, fill it 1cm deep then leave to chill and set. When cool, slice it up, lightly brush both sides with olive oil and either fry in a griddle pan over a medium heat or under a preheated medium grill until golden brown, about 2–3 minutes on each side.

Whisk the butter, Parmesan and some white or black pepper into the hot mixture, let the cheese melt, then taste and add more salt if necessary. At this point you could also whisk in some fresh herbs – chives, thyme, parsley, etc.

If the polenta becomes too thick you can thin it by stirring in some hot cream, milk or water. Serve hot with balls of your choice and plenty of sauce.

Mash Up

Why does mash taste so good when you go out to a restaurant? Because it is loaded with more butter and cream than you would ever believe you can put in at home, that's why. I am talking one whole pack of butter to a kilo of potatoes ... I won't do that here, but we will use a milk and cream combination as I like a soft mash. To soften the blow you can lose the cream and increase the milk ... or man up and lose the milk and increase the cream.

1kg floury potatoes

120ml double cream

120ml milk (optional – omit this if you prefer a firmer mash)

55g butter

salt and freshly ground black pepper

Wash the potatoes and place them in a large heavy-based pan. Cover them with cold water, add a teaspoon of salt and bring to the boil. Boil for approximately 20–30 minutes, or until they are soft and a fork can be inserted into them easily.

When the potatoes are not far off being ready, put the cream and milk into a pan and bring to boiling point.

Drain the potatoes and peel them when they are cool enough to be handled, then mash the flesh straight away, using a masher, fork or potato ricer for a fine consistency. Add the hot cream and milk, and the butter, beat in quickly, then continue to mash until you have a very smooth consistency. Add a good amount of salt and some twists of pepper to taste.

For Garlic Mash Up, beat in 6 Confit Garlic cloves and 50ml Confit Garlic oil (see page 155) when adding the butter.

In spring, if you're keen on a little foraging, pick some wild garlic leaves, thinly slice, then add them to the cream and milk as it boils and mash them in.

Potato Rösti

I love the mountains, and I try to escape there to ski, snowboard and walk as often as I can. In Chamonix I always enjoy getting stuck into the creamy, cheesy, layered potato dish tartiflette, and in Switzerland it's always been slabs of rösti. Don't turn the rösti over too early – you want it deliciously crispy on the outside and soft in the middle. Try adding bits of bacon, cheese and herbs to vary the dish.

2 tablespoons sunflower oil

1 small onion, chopped

750g waxy potatoes

50g butter (or 25g butter and 25g goose fat)

salt and freshly ground black pepper

Heat the oil in a heavy-based frying pan, then add the onion and cook for 5 minutes, or until the onion is soft and translucent but not browned.

Wash the potatoes, place them in a pan and cover with cold, salted water. Bring to the boil, then cook for 5 minutes, or until just tender. Drain and peel when cool enough to handle. Chill for at least 3 hours – the cold air of the fridge helps the potatoes to dry out and makes them easier to grate. If you are short of time you can crack on, but the rösti might not be quite as crispy.

Grate the potatoes coarsely into a bowl, then add the onion and season with salt and pepper.

Melt 25g of the butter in a heavy-based frying pan. Add the potato mixture and flatten into a cake. Cook over a low heat for 10 minutes, using a spatula to lift it occasionally to check the underside isn't burning.

Turn the rösti out on to a large plate. To do this, place your plate over the frying pan, hold the plate down firmly, then flip both over. You will end up with the cooked side of the rösti facing upwards on your plate. Melt the remaining butter in the pan and, once it is hot, slide the rösti back in, uncooked side down, and cook for a further 5–10 minutes.

A lovely golden rösti makes the perfect side to many ball dishes, but I love it topped with a fried egg and some Smokin' Bacon Balls (see page 41).

The Pudding Bowler

How can I make what is often considered a top comfort food the ULTIMATE comfort food?
This question popped into my head recently. Make the top Sunday roast accompaniment,
fill it with the top comfort food. Double top. (See page 61 for the result).

2 free-range eggs

200ml milk

100ml chilled water

110g plain flour

a large pinch of salt

vegetable oil or beef dripping

Whisk the eggs, milk and water together in a large bowl. Sieve the flour and add it gently to the liquid, whisking as you go so that you don't get any lumps. The batter should come together and be nice and silky smooth.

Cover with clingfilm and leave the batter for at least an hour to rest – in the fridge overnight is also fine. The longer the rest the higher the rise!

Preheat the oven to 220°C (425°F), Gas Mark 7.

Take a Yorkshire pudding tray with 8–10cm diameter moulds and fill each with half a teaspoon of oil or beef dripping. Put the tray into the oven for 10 minutes to let the oil get nice and hot. Once hot, carefully pour in the batter two-thirds of the way up each mould. Bake them until they have risen and are golden brown, about 20 minutes.

To serve, fill each pudding bowl with a spoonful of mash (pick a flavour) or some small rustic roast potatoes, then choose your ball and ladle over some sauce for the ultimate comfort food. I love the Lamb, Rosemary & Garlic Meatballs (see page 60) with Red Wine Gravy (see page 90), or The Rose Bowl veal and Parmesan balls (see page 51) with Wild Mushroom Sauce (see page 92).

Puy Lentil Salad with Avocado, Halloumi & Walnuts

Lentils provide an earthy base for a number of salad and side variations. Cook them slowly, and always add the vinaigrette or dressing after draining when they are still warm, as they absorb the flavour much better then. I've used slices of chargrilled halloumi here, but feta, goat's cheese and mozzarella all work well, too.

225g Puy lentils

a little olive oil, for frying

1 onion, sliced

1 garlic clove, crushed

1 large carrot, peeled and cut into large chunks

3 sprigs each of thyme and parsley

1 bay leaf

1 tablespoon olive oil

1 tablespoon cider vinegar

1 tablespoon soy sauce

2 tablespoons chopped flat-leaf parsley

250g halloumi cheese, cut into 1cm thick slices

2 tablespoons pomegranate molasses

2 tablespoons walnut oil

2 tablespoons extra virgin olive oil

1 romaine lettuce, cut into chunks

1 ripe avocado, sliced

4 tablespoons Caramelized Red Onions (see page 154)

3 tablespoons walnuts, roughly chopped

1 lime, cut into wedges

salt and freshly ground black pepper

Wash the lentils in cold water, then rinse and drain. Heat a little oil in a heavy-based pan. Add the onion and fry for 2 minutes, then add the garlic and cook gently until the onion begins to turn golden. Add the carrot, thyme, parsley sprigs and bay leaf, stir, then add the lentils and cover them with cold water.

Bring to the boil, then turn the heat down to a simmer. Simmer for 20 minutes, or until the lentils have absorbed the water and are soft yet retain some bite. Add a little more boiling water if you need to. Remove the pan from the heat and drain the lentils, removing the carrot and herbs. Let the lentils stand for 5 minutes, then stir in the olive oil, vinegar, soy sauce and chopped parsley. Taste for seasoning, remembering that the halloumi will be salty to taste.

Fry the halloumi slices in a dry pan or griddle them until they turn golden and soften.

Mix together the pomegranate molasses, walnut oil and extra virgin olive oil to make a dressing and add a little salt and pepper.

Add the lettuce and avocado to the lentils and toss with half the dressing. Arrange on a platter or individual plates, with the halloumi and caramelized onions on top. Pour over the rest of the dressing, sprinkle over the walnuts, then season and serve either warm, or at room temperature.

This makes a great lunch on its own or with a side of Beef & Chorizo Balls (see page 28), Great Balls of Fire (see page 34) or Smokin' Bacon Balls (see page 41).

Lowry & Baker's Chicory, Stilton, Pear & Pecan Salad

When I was developing the first few meatballs, and dreaming about balling in public, I thought it would be a good idea to road-test a few recipes, but I needed a space. Tucked away at the top of Portobello Road in west London is a gem of a café called Lowry & Baker. The owners, Katy and Maya, kindly agreed to give me the keys to their café for one night, so we popped up, rolled up, called it 'Portoballo' and opened the doors to a few friends. Visit www.thebowleruk.tumblr.com/movies to get a flavour of the night and see the café. This is one of Lowry & Baker's delicious salads, which makes a great side.

1 large handful of pecan nuts, shelled

200g mixed baby leaves (such as baby spinach, ruby chard and wild rocket)

2 ripe pears

a squeeze of lemon juice

2 heads of red chicory

200g good-quality Stilton cheese (such as Colston Bassett)

4 tablespoons extra virgin olive oil

1 tablespoon white wine vinegar

1 teaspoon Dijon mustard

1 teaspoon real maple syrup

a pinch of salt and freshly ground black pepper

Heat the oven to 160°C (325°F), Gas Mark 3.

Put the pecan nuts on a baking tray and toast them in the oven for about 10 minutes, or until you start to smell them toasting. Remove from the oven and allow to cool.

Place the baby leaves in a large mixing bowl. Cut the pears into quarters lengthways and remove the core. Slice finely lengthways and add to the bowl. Squeeze over a little lemon juice to stop them discolouring.

Cut the chicory widthways, pull apart the leaves and add to the bowl. Crumble in the Stilton, then add the pecan nuts.

For the dressing, combine the oil, vinegar, mustard, maple syrup, salt and pepper in a jar with a lid and shake well to mix. Pour the dressing over the salad and toss everything together gently.

Divide between four nice plates and serve. I love it with Smokin' Bacon Balls (see page 41).

Jerusalem Artichoke Gratin

I love Jerusalem artichokes. They are a little secret weapon in my home cooking armoury.
Not many people buy them, so when you use them to make soup or even chips, more often
than not you hit the target and people remark about the interesting flavour.
Here I've layered them alongside some potatoes in classic gratin style. This cooking technique
works with a lot of root vegetables, so feel free to experiment.

250ml double cream

250ml milk

1 garlic clove

juice of ½ a lemon

350g floury potatoes, peeled

350g Jerusalem artichokes, peeled

1 leek, sliced

30g butter

**salt and freshly ground
black pepper**

Put the cream, milk and the garlic clove into a large pan and bring to the
boil. Remove from the heat and set aside to cool, to allow the garlic to infuse.

Meanwhile, fill a bowl with cold water and add the lemon juice. Slice the
potatoes and artichokes into 3mm rounds. Drop the slices of artichoke
into the bowl of lemon water as you go – this will prevent them discolouring.

Preheat the oven to 160°C (325°F), Gas Mark 3.

Grease an ovenproof dish with a little of the butter and arrange a layer
of potato slices, slightly overlapping each other, in the base. Season with
salt and pepper, then add a layer of artichoke slices and season again.
Seasoning each layer as you go, sprinkle over the leeks, then add another
layer of artichokes and finish with a layer of potatoes. Remove the garlic
clove, then pour the cream mixture over the gratin so that it just covers the
last potato layer and push down gently. Dot the rest of the butter over the top.

Bake in the oven for about 1 hour, or until golden brown and bubbling
around the edges. If the top looks like its browning too quickly, cover it
with a piece of foil to prevent it burning.

I eat this gratin by itself, hot or cold. It also works well with a large number
of balls, especially Pork & Fennel Meatballs (see page 16), Ball Shiitake
(see page 27) and The Popeye (see page 36).

Nutty Bulgar Wheat Salad

Bulgar wheat is used a lot in tabbouleh, but is often overlooked as a tasty side.
You can combine a lot of ingredients with it to create a fresh-tasting salad to accompany
your favourite balls. Great with Beef & Chorizo Balls (see page 28) or at a barbecue with
skewered Balls on the Line (see page 24).

**500ml Chicken Stock (see page 90)
or vegetable stock**

**1 garlic clove, peeled and squashed
with the flat of a knife**

2 sprigs of thyme

200g bulgar wheat

20g currants

**75g pecan nuts, chopped
(or walnuts)**

1 red onion, finely sliced

juice of 1 lemon

2 tablespoons olive oil

**2 tablespoons chopped
flat-leaf parsley**

2 tablespoons chopped mint

sea salt flakes

Put the stock into a pan with the garlic and thyme. Bring to the boil, then
reduce the heat and simmer for 2 minutes to let the flavours infuse a little.

Put the bulgar wheat and currants into a bowl. Remove the garlic and
thyme from the stock and pour it over the bulgar wheat. Let the wheat
absorb the liquid for a few minutes while it cools a little. Stir in the pecan
nuts, onion, lemon juice, olive oil, parsley and mint.

Season with a couple of pinches of sea salt flakes and serve underneath
your chosen balls with your favourite sauce and some peppery salad leaves.

Courgette, Chickpea & Feta Salad

This is a great salad for barbecuers and ballers alike. It's hearty enough to make a stand-alone 'meal in one' as well as being a good accompaniment to balls.

1 x 400g tin of chickpeas, drained, or 50g dried chickpeas, soaked overnight

2 tablespoons olive oil

1 red onion, sliced

2 garlic cloves, crushed

1 red chilli, seeds removed, sliced

1 teaspoons thyme leaves

zest and juice of 1 lime

200g feta cheese

4 courgettes, green and yellow if possible

200g baby leaf salad (such as watercress, spinach, red chard)

THE DRESSING

4 tablespoons Confit Garlic oil (see page 155), or olive oil

2 tablespoons white wine vinegar

2 teaspoons honey

salt and freshly ground black pepper

If using soaked dried chickpeas, drain them, put them into a large pan, cover them with three times their volume of water and bring to the boil. Simmer partially covered for 2 hours, testing after this time to see that they are soft but retain a little bite. Drain and allow to cool.

Heat the oil in a heavy-based frying pan over a medium heat. Add the red onion and cook on low for 2 minutes, then add the garlic, chilli, thyme leaves and a pinch of salt. Cook for another 4 minutes, or until the onion is soft and translucent, then add the chickpeas and leave to simmer for 5 minutes, stirring occasionally and adding the lime zest and half the juice for the last couple of minutes. Check the seasoning, crumble in the feta and set aside to cool to room temperature.

Meanwhile, wash and dry the courgettes. Using a vegetable peeler, peel off strips of courgette lengthways down one side, coming in as close as you can to the central core, then turn and do the same to the other side. You should get strips with green or yellow skin on the edges.

Put a griddle pan over a high heat. When it's hot, brush a few of the larger strips of courgette with a little oil and lay them lengthways in the pan. Chargrill the courgette strips on one side until you get griddle marks, then turn them over and do the same on the other side.

Bring a pan of salted water to the boil, drop the remaining courgette strips in for 1 minute, then drain and refresh under cold water.

Put all the dressing ingredients into a jam jar and shake to combine.

Put the baby leaves into a bowl and toss with a little of the dressing so that they are lightly coated. Arrange the courgettes in a serving dish, put the baby leaves on top, and pile the chickpea and feta mix on top of that.

Serve with Baa Baa Balls (see page 56) for a double feta hit.

Spicy Slaw

I hate limp, acidic, carrot-laden coleslaw. It was served so often on the side of a
jacket potato at school that it almost put me off for life. However, if you up the quality
of the ingredients and give it a bit of time to let the flavours combine, a crunchy, rich
coleslaw can work really well with a lot of meatball recipes.
I suggest you make your own mayonnaise, though any type of mayo you have to hand
will work. Feel free to substitute a different type of chilli for the jalapeños.

¼ of a red cabbage, core removed

¼ of a white cabbage, core removed

1 teaspoon sugar

2 spring onions, finely sliced

1 tablespoon finely chopped red
jalapeño peppers (you can use the
ones in a jar if you can't find fresh)

1 tablespoon finely chopped
coriander, leaves and stalks
separated

75g Real Mayonnaise (see page 115)

75g soured cream

2 teaspoons wholegrain mustard

juice of ½ a lemon

2 teaspoons cider vinegar

1 teaspoon sea salt

½ teaspoon freshly ground
black pepper

Finely slice the cabbage quarters – you can use a mandolin for this, but
mind those fingers. Put the cabbage into a large bowl, sprinkle over the
sugar and stir, then add the spring onions, jalapeños and coriander stalks
and mix together.

In a separate bowl combine the mayonnaise, soured cream, mustard, lemon
juice, cider vinegar, salt and pepper, then pour this dressing over the veg
and toss gently to combine.

If you really have to tuck in immediately, go ahead, but I prefer to cover the
bowl with clingfilm and refrigerate it for 1–24 hours, to allow the flavours to
mingle. Scatter over the coriander leaves just before serving. This works by
the side of many balls to give a dish a bit of crunch.

Citrus Couscous

This couscous is a meal in itself. Some people reckon couscous is bland, but I think it can
be the backing band to a load of wonderful solo ingredients. This is great alongside the
Baa Baa Balls (see page 56) and can be spiced up with some harissa.

80ml extra virgin olive oil

1 onion, finely chopped

1 garlic clove, crushed

½ teaspoon dried chilli flakes

250g couscous

500ml boiling water

3 tablespoons pine nuts

seeds from 1 pomegranate

3 tablespoons finely chopped mint

**3 tablespoons finely chopped
flat-leaf parsley**

juice of 1 orange

juice and finely grated zest of 1 lime

**sea salt flakes and freshly ground
black pepper**

Heat the oil in a large heavy-based pan. Add the onion and cook on a
low heat for 2 minutes. Add the garlic and cook for a further 5 minutes,
or until the onion is soft and translucent. Then add the chilli flakes
to the oil, stir and set aside.

Put the couscous into a large bowl and stir in the boiling water.
Add ½ teaspoon of salt, then cover the bowl with clingfilm and leave
for 10 minutes.

Meanwhile, heat a dry frying pan over a medium heat and add the pine
nuts. Toast them until they are golden, keeping them moving around the
pan so that they don't burn. Once toasted, put them into a bowl.

Split the pomegranate in half around the equator, then hold cut side
down over a bowl and tap vigorously with the back of a wooden spoon –
the seeds should dislodge and fall into the bowl. Don't perform this near
any new white carpets or sofas.

Add the rest of the ingredients to the couscous and mix with a fork to fluff
it up and separate the grains. Taste, adjust the seasoning and serve.

Unless you're serving it with the Baa Baa Balls, you can crumble in some
feta or goat's cheese, too.

Pickled Carrot & Daikon

A daikon looks like a huge white carrot. Also called mooli, this large Asian radish can be eaten raw or cooked. It's great shredded and mixed with Citrus Ponzu (see page 113), julienned, stir-fried, thrown into a curry or pickled as it is here.

250g carrots

250g daikon, woody bits removed

1 teaspoon salt

40g caster sugar

125ml warm water

160ml rice vinegar

Julienne the carrot and daikon by slicing thinly lengthways, then chopping them into matchsticks.

Dissolve the salt and sugar in the warm water. Stir in the vinegar. Put the carrots and daikon into a jar and pour over the pickling liquor, making sure the vegetables are covered. Seal the jar and refrigerate for at least an hour before using. It's best eaten after 3 days, and will keep in the fridge for up to 2 weeks.

●●●●●●●●

Pickled Cucumber

This recipe gives the cucumber a sweet and sour taste, with a crunchy bite.
I use it as a relish when I serve my meatballs Bap 'n' Ball style (see page 29) in sliders
or alongside Björn Balls (see page 46).

150g soft light brown sugar,
or golden caster sugar

150ml cider vinegar, or white
wine vinegar

30g salt

2 cucumbers, sliced into 3–5mm
rounds (around 500g in total – any
more and the liquid won't cover them)

4 banana shallots, sliced, or 1 large
onion, quartered and finely sliced

Put the sugar, vinegar and salt into a bowl and whisk together. Add the cucumbers and shallots, stir, then cover the bowl and refrigerate for at least 4 hours. Transfer to a sterilized jar – they will keep in the fridge for up to 1–2 weeks.

Honey-roasted Vegetables

This is a simple way to cook vegetables, with the honey glaze enhancing their sweetness.
There are no real rules, just adjust the type of veg and the quantities and roast the same way.
Don't over-cook the veg, though – you should be able to insert a knife easily into them, but
at the same time they should retain a little bite.

1 sweet potato, peeled, halved and cut into 2cm chunks (you can use butternut squash or pumpkin if you prefer it not too sweet)

2 red onions, cut into 2cm chunks

1 red or yellow pepper, seeds removed, cut into 2cm squares

2 carrots, sliced diagonally 1cm thick

2 courgettes, sliced diagonally 1cm thick

2 tablespoons olive oil

2 tablespoons clear honey

leaves from 3 sprigs of thyme

4 tablespoons toasted pine nuts (optional)

sea salt and freshly ground black pepper

Preheat the oven to 220°C (425°F), Gas Mark 7.

Put all the vegetables into a roasting tin or ovenproof dish that can take them easily. Drizzle them with the olive oil and half the honey, then sprinkle with the thyme and season with salt and pepper.

Roast the veg for 12 minutes, then give them a shake, add the remaining honey and roast for a further 5–10 minutes. Take out of the oven and stir in the pine nuts, if using.

These roasted veg are great with many of the balls in this book, especially Lamb, Rosemary & Garlic Meatballs (see page 60), as well as alongside roasts, or simply served on top of couscous with some goat's cheese.

Asian Greens

'Always eat your greens …' as we were constantly being told when we were little. Now I can't get enough of them, cooked the Asian way with lashings of chilli, ginger and garlic. It's the fast way to get five-a-day. They complement many of the meatballs in this book, so they're the perfect side.

450g greens (a mix of pak choi, purple sprouting broccoli, gai lan and green beans)

1 tablespoon sunflower oil

1 teaspoon grated fresh ginger

1 green or red chilli, seeds removed, finely sliced

1 spring onion, finely sliced

1 garlic clove, crushed

1 tablespoon soy sauce

2 teaspoons sesame oil

Steam the vegetables over a pan of boiling water until just tender. Pak choi will take 2 minutes, sprouting broccoli, gai lan and green beans will take up to 5 minutes.

Heat the sunflower oil in a wok or a large heavy-based frying pan over a high heat. Add the ginger, chilli and the white part of the spring onion and stir-fry for 1 minute in the hot oil. Add the garlic, stirring constantly to make sure that nothing catches and burns, then add the steamed greens and the soy sauce and toss gently to coat.

Add the sesame oil at the end and serve immediately, with the green part of the spring onion scattered on top.

Caramelized Red Onions

This is a simple way to really enrich and intensify the flavour of red onions. I often make a large batch and keep them in the fridge, for adding to salads, omelettes, burgers and balls.

60ml olive oil (or 75ml if using the oven method)

350g red onions, sliced

2 tablespoons brown sugar (optional)

1 tablespoon balsamic vinegar (optional)

salt and freshly ground black pepper

STOVETOP METHOD

Heat the oil in a large heavy-based pan. Add the onions along with a twist of salt and pepper and cook on a low heat, stirring occasionally, for 30–45 minutes, or until they are golden brown and sticky in appearance.

You can substitute white onions for red, and add 2 tablespoons of brown sugar and 1 tablespoon of balsamic vinegar 10 minutes before the end of the cooking time if you like.

OVEN METHOD

To make larger quantities, you can spread the onions on a baking tray, cover with the oil, sugar, vinegar, salt and pepper, and bake at 160°C (325°F), Gas Mark 3 for 45 minutes, giving them a little check and stir halfway through, or until caramelized and sweet and sour to taste.

● ● ● ● ● ● ● ●

Preparation time: **35** minutes Cooking time: **5** minutes Serves **8+** as a garnish

Crispy Fried Shallots

I sprinkle these crispy devils on top of the Green Chilli Chicken Balls (see page 52), but they are a great garnish for many dishes. They keep well in a sealed jar.

6 shallots, finely sliced

1 teaspoon salt

500ml water

60ml vegetable oil

If you have time, it's a good idea to toss the shallots in the salt, pour over the water and leave for 30 minutes – it helps give them that extra crunch. If you are in a hurry, though, you can skip this step.

Pour the oil into a heavy-based pan or wok over a medium heat. Drain and rinse the shallots and dry them thoroughly. When the oil is hot, add the shallots and fry for 2–3 minutes, or until they turn golden brown and crispy. Watch them like a hawk as you want them to caramelize, not burn.

Take them out of the oil with a slotted spoon and drain on kitchen paper. Either use immediately or let them cool down, then transfer them to a clean jam jar to use at a later date.

Confit Garlic

Confit is a way of preserving that is most often associated with meats, in which they are cooked in their own fat. Duck leg confit is the best-known example – duck legs are cooked slowly in duck fat and then allowed to cool, the fat enveloping the meat to preserve it. Here I've slowly cooked garlic in oil, which makes the cloves tender and sweet, with the oil becoming garlic-infused.

3 bulbs of garlic (about 30 cloves), peeled, with the brown root end cut off

250ml olive oil

There are two ways of doing this. The first is to put the garlic and oil into a large heavy-based pan into which the garlic will fit comfortably in one layer, making sure it is completely covered by the oil. Heat the oil gently until small bubbles start to form, then turn the heat down to low. You don't want the oil to boil, as this is all about low and slow, and you don't want to brown the garlic. A heat diffusion mat is good for this, to stop the oil getting too hot, otherwise you'll have to take the pan on and off the heat every time it looks as though it's getting hot enough for the garlic to brown.

Cook, checking regularly, for 30–60 minutes. You are looking to get it to a soft consistency, so that you can pierce it easily with a knife or squish it against the side of the pan.

The second way to confit the garlic is to heat the oven to 150°C (300°F), Gas Mark 2. Get an ovenproof dish, put a single layer of garlic in it, cover it with oil and slowly cook for 45 minutes to 1 hour until the garlic is soft, as described above.

Once the garlic is cooked, turn off the heat and let the pan or dish cool down. Remove the cloves with a fork or a slotted spoon and put them into a sterilized jar, then pour over the oil and refrigerate for up to 4 weeks (you won't keep it that long, though, because it is too good not to use). The oil is perfect for using in dressings and mayonnaise, for drizzling on pizzas, and the cloves can be stirred into mash and sauces.

Bean Balls

Surprise and apologies, but these balls aren't made from beans at all.
I met Bean Sopwith in an earlier life – she even lent me her flat to do some meatball prep
once. Whenever we're talking food she's always suggesting ingredients and alternatives to
make things healthier, protein-enriched and all round super-foodier. Bean is a nutrition and
behavioural change expert. She's kindly come up with a super-fuel snack ball we can all make
and eat on the go – in between meals, at school, or a couple of hours before an exercise
session. Ready for a ballsy, health food hit …

100g creamed coconut block
(for a healthier alternative,
use 50g coconut oil plus a 3cm
square of creamed coconut block
melted with a little hot water)

175g organic nut butter
(the best is almond)

125g oats (or use pumpkin seeds,
soaked overnight, for a low-carb
alternative)

75g palm sugar (see * for
alternative healthier sweeteners)

50g desiccated coconut (optional),
plus extra for rolling

60g cacao powder

1 teaspoon ground cinnamon

125ml blueberries (optional)

2 teaspoons vanilla extract

Melt the coconut block (with the coconut oil, if using) in a pan over a low
heat. Then either process all the ingredients together in a food processor
or mix them together by hand in a bowl.

Line a small shallow dish with baking paper and roll the mixture into about
35 balls each about 3cm in diameter. This can be a bit messy, so it's best
to keep your hands cool by dipping them frequently into cold water. Pour
some desiccated coconut on to a plate, then roll the balls in it to coat and
place on a baking tray.

Freeze for 1 hour to harden the balls up, then store in the fridge. Best
eaten straight from the fridge, served with fresh blueberries, meringues
and a bit of cream for an alternative dessert. Move over, Eton Mess.

Now wow your friends down the pub with these factoids from Bean:
'These balls are better than most convenience snack foods because
they contain healthy fats and proteins that don't over-stimulate insulin
production, and are therefore less likely to cause weight gain and give a
more consistent energy output. Four balls is a healthy meal replacement,
especially useful when on the road and healthy options are limited. If all
petrol stations sold these balls, there would be some happier, healthier
travellers on the road. Maybe we could reduce some road rage with raw balls.'

* Healthy sweeteners: Most supermarkets now stock natural sweeteners
made from plant extracts, including xylitol (found in berries and fruit),
and stevia, a natural sweetener extracted from the herbal plant, available
in most health food stores in granules or as a liquid, although the best
quality is purchased online – www.stevia-de.com. You can also use ZSweet,
date syrup, maple syrup or wild honey – all available at larger health food
stores. Avoid agave, as this is not a health food. There are lots of websites
which sell these products online if your local health food store doesn't
stock them, including www.red23.co.uk.

Index

Author's Acknowledgements

I feel incredibly lucky to have been given the opportunity to write this book. There are loads of people to thank, those who physically put the book together, but also all those that helped me get The Bowler to a place where a book was even a viable proposition. It's going to be long, but it's important. Huge thanks and respect to all those who queue on cold, rain sodden, February lunchtimes and all those who set up your stalls, hours before the lunchtimes begin. Without your support, passion and dedication this wouldn't have been possible.

Thank you to everyone at Smart Hospitality whose help on every level has been unfathomable. Robin Bidgood for listening at the start, and the pep talks along the way, Greg Lawson for his time and knowledge, David Ridgway for his 'calm under pressure' and 'nothing's a problem' attitude – a true gent.

To head chef Rhys 'Grhys-ball' Janzin for inspiration and passing on the tricks of the trade. Matthew Hughes, Jonny Hannan, Zoe Wager, Simon Read, Ryan Potter and Richard Gee for putting up with, and answering, all my inane questions. Fabian, Dorothy, Nick, Leon, Rob, Tom, David and everyone else, you know who you are. Seriously, when you're a lone ball slinger, seeing your friendly faces is a real boost and comfort.

Thanks to Gary Bentley, Lee and everyone at the butchers, Bentleys of Surrey. Passion, knowledge and knife skills. To allow me to work alongside you, and not make the tea, is truly generous.

Andy Ashton who gave me my first chance at being a baller back in 2011 and when I tried to get out of it forcing me to do the event. To Petra Barran of KERB (formally Eat.St) who is busy championing food on the streets as we speak. Hannah Norris from Nourish PR for her insider industry knowledge and help with getting the book out there. Jonathan Downey for Tweat'ing up and supporting the scene. Ghislain Pascal for his no nonsense advice, life support and letting me loose in The Imperial Arms kitchen. Thanks to the marketeers who take on the spaces and take time to negotiate places for us to trade. Noticeably Toby Allen for setting up the wonderful Brockley Market and Dom Cools-Lartigue for night market, Street Feast London.

Algy Batten, Mark McConnachie and the team at Fivefootsix. Not only did they kick my arse to get things going but their initial design and branding skills launched The Bowler. Thanks also for putting a roof over my head in years gone by.

My niece Nia Felwick, god-daughter Mathilda Douglas and Ottilie Douglas for agreeing to demonstrate their rolling skills for the book. You're beautiful.

To Alison Starling at Octopus Publishing for literally getting the ball rolling, thinking there's a book in them balls and assembling a team to create something above and beyond expectation. To Sybella Stephens for editing and cracking the whip so I got everything in (almost on time), and Juliette Norsworthy for designing such a beautiful book. Catherine Phipps for helpful comments on my recipes, and Annie Rigg for making a series of spheres look so different. Abigail Read whose ball-point pen and pencil skills produced the beautiful and quirky illustrations. Cris Barnett, your genius photography speaks for itself. Thank you for taking the project on, you're the best vegetarian option I've come across.

Thanks also to Dan Stephings, Jim Greayer, Chris McIntosh, Toby Allen, Louis Fernando, Andrew Ager and Roberto Ruiz (ruizherrera.com) for the addional photography on the endpapers.

To my friends who have stuck with me over the years. You know who you are. I'm very lucky to have such an amazing group of brothers and sisters, and genuinely, without your support, encouragement and help The Bowler would not be rolling.

Shouts go out to the ballers. Those of you that have been baptised in spicy tomato sauce and helped to sell. Bertie 'my balls, your mouth, five pounds' Ager, Matthew 'Kiwi Matt' Goodwin and Jim 'nice Swedish meatball snaps' Greayer. Dan Stephings for both balling and last minute design and photography and Gavin Douglas for his cabbage slicing on Eat.St and the rest.

A special mention for Daniel Johnson-Allen who gave up his weekends in the early days to make sure I got settled. I cannot thank you enough.

And the family. Mum and Dad, you are an inspiration, full of life, love and passion. Your support for everything I've ever done, and the stable home you created for us, provides a strong base, where jumping into something new becomes easier, knowing whatever happens there will be a hug, cuppa, slice and kind words, ready to comfort. My brother Matt and little sis (in-law) Siân. Clever, kind and caring. Thanks for all your advice and sublime Sunday roasts. Matt, it's always good to see your friendly face at Eat.St and thanks from all the traders for eating your way along the road.

And finally the biggest thanks goes to my wonderful wife Rachel who puts food on the table when I've been too busy to eat, comforts me in times of extreme tiredness and stress, and turns out to ball when noone else can make it. Thanks for everything, with love.

Roll on.